T0023971

LISBON

Like a Local

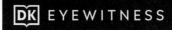

LISBON
Like a Local

BY THE PEOPLE WHO CALL IT HOME

Contents

NIGHTLIFE

OUTDOORS

meet the locals

LUCY BRYSON

After learning the lingo in Rio de Janeiro, Lucy traded drizzly Manchester for sunny Lisbon in 2015. A writer and editor from 9 to 5, Lucy spends her free time honing her downward dog and drinking the local vinho – not simultaneously!

REUBEN ROSS

Reuben's love affair with Lisbon started when he moved here to study for his doctorate. When he's not nosing through history books, Reuben explores the city with his camera in hand, stopping for a coffee and pastel de nata along the way.

JOANA TABORDA

Born and bred in Lisbon, Joana splits her time between the city and the island of Madeira. She's passionate about her home town and has made a career out of writing about it. Work aside, Joana loves learning new crafts and trying out the latest craft brews (she seriously knows her beer).

Lisbon

WELCOME TO THE CITY

You don't have to have been born in Lisbon to be a Lisboeta. Portugal's capital is home to generations of immigrants from its former empire, digital nomads lured by the laid-back lifestyle and folks who fell in love with Lisbon after just one life-changing visit.

And it's not hard to see why this stunner of a city has stolen so many hearts. Pastel-pretty houses with terracotta roofs tumble down to the sparkling Tejo and even the tightest of alleyways is adorned with *azulejos* and *calçadas*. Time moves slowly here – trams trundle through the streets, crafters carefully consider their latest project and locals linger over cups of coffee and bottles of wine (usually while soaking up the views from one of the many *miradouros*).

It all sounds rather dreamy, doesn't it? But let's not forget the many hardships that Lisboetas have faced over the years, from earthquakes to dictatorships to financial crises. You can always rely on the locals to meet challenges head on, though. This is a city of quiet reinvention, where munitions factories are transformed into cutting-edge cultural spaces, car parks are topped with edgy rooftop bars and once-abandoned *quiosques* have been reclaimed as daily hangouts.

And that's where this book will take you. Inside these pages, Lisbon locals reveal a side of their city that flies under the radar. Of course, you'll still find all the beaches and *pastelarias* you've dreamed of (who can resist those creamy custard tarts?). But you'll also discover off-beat galleries, whispered-about craft breweries and pint-sized bookshops that barely fit one customer.

Whether you're already head over heels for Lisbon or about to make your first visit, this book will help you discover a cooler side of this sunny city. Enjoy Lisbon, but do it the local way.

Liked by the locals

"Lisbon fills you with a sense of wonder. You never know what you're going to find around the corner: a secret bar, a tiled façade or a glimpse of the river. There's no better place to get lost."

JOANA TABORDA, TRAVEL WRITER

The sun shines on lucky Lisbon for much of the year, but the city still has distinct seasons, each with its own traditions and events.

Lisbon
THROUGH THE YEAR

SPRING

ALFRESCO EVERYTHING
As soon as the winter chill loses its bite, Lisboetas take their social gatherings outdoors, catching up over cups of coffee (or cocktails) and plates of *petiscos* at *quiosques*, pavement cafés and *miradouros*.

CARNIVAL CAPERS
To mark the beginning of Lent, locals follow jubilant *blocos* (street bands) around the city for five days of unapologetic partying.

JOYOUS JACARANDAS
Late spring sees Lisbon coloured purple as thousands of jacaranda trees burst into bloom. This spectacular sight never gets old and even the longest-time residents still pause to admire the tunnels of violet trees.

SUMMER

SAINTS, SARDINES AND SANGRIA
June's Festas dos Santos Populares (Popular Saints' Festival) signals the start of summer. During this fun-filled fortnight, revellers chow down on freshly grilled sardines, sip fruity sangria and dance till dawn to *pimba* (Portuguese pop music).

PARK LIFE
When the mercury soars, the whole city seems to descend on the city's parks and gardens. Here, neighbours stop their

strolls to chat, students gather for impromptu kickabouts and jam sessions, and friends toast the good weather.

SNAIL-CENTRIC SOCIALIZING

Love them or loathe them, there's no escaping snails in summer. At the height of the season, almost every restaurant has a sign outside proclaiming *"temos caraóis"* (we have snails) and this salty dish becomes the go-to order.

AUTUMN

SPECTACULAR SUNDOWNERS

The city's rooftop bars enjoy a last hurrah in autumn when Lisbon's sunsets grow ever more spectacular. After work, groups of friends throw on hoodies and light jackets, and head to their local *miradouro* to catch the free show.

"TECH GLASTONBURY"

Techies rule the city for four days each November. During WebSummit (aka "Tech Glastonbury"), late-night networking events take over the city's hottest bars and restaurants, especially around Parque das Nações, where the conference moved from Dublin in 2016.

CULTURAL HAPPENINGS

When those long, lazy beach days have faded to a distant memory, Lisboetas head indoors for a dose of culture. The curious check out the latest exhibitions, plays and crafty classes.

WINTER

WALKING IN A LISBON WONDERLAND

Wrapped-up couples and families swarm to Parque Eduardo VII for Wonderland Lisboa – Portugal's largest Christmas festival. Here, they pick up gifts, skate on the ice rink and ride the Ferris wheel.

NEW YEAR'S EVE

While some Lisboetas gather in Praça do Comércio to watch the Réveillon (New Year's Eve) fireworks over the Tejo, just as many head to house parties to watch the show on TV.

WINTER WARMERS

Lisboetas' homes are designed to keep cool during the summer, rather than warm in winter. To escape the chill, locals retreat to cosy restaurants and busy bars, picking up freshly roasted chestnuts and hot, spiced wine on the way.

There's an art to being a Lisboeta, from the dos and don'ts at quiosques *to riding the city's trams. Here's a breakdown of all you need to know.*

Lisbon

KNOW-HOW

For a directory of health and safety resources, safe spaces, and accessibility information, turn to page 186. For everything else, read on.

EAT

Eating breakfast on the hoof is standard in Lisbon but lunch and dinner are firmly sit-down affairs. Most Lisboetas take a full hour for lunch, served from 1pm to 3pm. Dinners are eaten no earlier than 8pm, with kitchens closing around 11pm.

Booking is rarely necessary, except for the fanciest of restaurants, and there's never a need to dress up.

DRINK

Locals take advantage of their sunny city and drink outside as much as possible, whether beside a *quiosque*, at a rooftop bar or even in the street. In the morning, Lisboetas order a *bica*, which

is a bit like an espresso. For a drop of milk, ask for a *café pingado*, while a latte is a *meia de leite*.

Wine and beer are acceptable from noon. Pints are strictly for tourists; locals order an *imperial* (a small draught beer) or a bottle. In some bars and restaurants, a glass of wine is cheaper than a soft drink. Pace yourself – locals drink, but rarely too much.

SHOP

Online shopping has yet to take off in Lisbon, so locals spend a lot of time (and we mean a lot of time) physically deliberating over everything from fresh food to vintage clothes. Shops are generally open from 10am to 8pm, though they often close earlier on Sundays. As you now know, lunch is a sacred time, and smaller businesses may close from around 1pm to 3pm.

Markets are usually held on weekends only. Bear in mind that haggling isn't really the done thing. Oh, and it's always worth carrying a tote bag to avoid the charge for a plastic one.

ARTS & CULTURE
Lucky Lisboetas can score free tickets to many of the city's museums and galleries on Sundays and public holidays, but visitors will need to fork out €8–15 for admission. There's no need to book ahead, but non-residents might want to avoid the weekend crowds by visiting between Tuesday and Friday (many places close on Mondays). Evening entertainment is similarly relaxed.

NIGHTLIFE
Lisboetas don't rush their nights out – when the party lasts from dusk till dawn, there's no need to. It all kicks off with a shop-bought sundowner in a park or at a *miradouro*. Then it's time for a slow crawl around Bairro Alto or Cais do Sodré's bars. Most clubs open around midnight, but nobody turns up until 2am. Some clubs have tough door policies, so check out the vibes and dress to match.

OUTDOORS
When the sun's out (which is often), Lisboetas flock to the city's parks,

miradouros and surrounding beaches. Don't be surprised if you see many topless or semi-nude locals working on their tan – it's a perfectly acceptable practice. Be sure to pick up your rubbish, as littering carries a hefty fine.

Keep in mind

Here are some tips and tidbits that will help you fit in like a local.

» **Keep cash handy** Some small businesses won't accept international cards, so always carry some cash.

» **Smoking** Smoking inside is a big no-no. If you have to light up, do it outside.

» **Tip if you like** It's polite to tip waiters and taxi drivers (to the nearest euro), but it's not obligatory.

» **Stay hydrated** Lisbon is home to hundreds of free drinking fountains, and plenty of cafés, bars and restaurants will be happy to refill your water bottle – just ask nicely.

GETTING AROUND

Lisbon is divided into 24 *freguesias* (administrative regions), which are each made up of several *bairros* (neighbourhoods, p14). There's a marked difference between the layout of the upper and lower reaches of the city: Baixa (or downtown) is neatly set out in a grid formation, while the loftier neighbourhoods, like Alfama and Bairro Alto, have a higgledy-piggledy layout of steep, narrow streets. Use the Tejo (or Tagus) as a reference point when exploring Lisbon's labyrinthine upper echelons – all roads downhill eventually lead to the river.

To get you to the right place, we've provided what3words addresses for each sight in this book, meaning you can quickly pinpoint exactly where you're heading.

On foot

Despite the hills and maze of streets, walking is a great way to see Lisbon in all its glory. You can explore the tiniest of *becos* (alleyways) and pause at *miradouros* for as long as you please. Nobody's ever in much of a hurry here – and why would they be? Even so, be kind to the locals and step to the side if you want to stop to take pictures or check directions. We won't blame you

for getting distracted by a great view or pretty *azulejos* but stay sharp and keep an eye out for tram rails. Lastly, wear the right shoes – there's no place for heels or slick soles on the city's steep and slippery *calçadas* (tiled pavements).

On wheels

Thanks to a flurry of competing bike-sharing schemes and ongoing investment in new cycle lanes (60 km/ 37 miles and counting), Lisbon is getting better when it comes to cycling. Gira is the original and top bike-sharing scheme, with hundreds of docking stations around town. Renting one of their 1,400 bikes will set you back €2 per day, with an additional charge per 45-minute ride. Simply download the app to get started.

But what about the hills? We hear you and don't worry: e-bikes are widely available. Plus, if you get tired of pedalling, you can take your wheels on the train, metro or ferries for free outside of rush hour.

Helmets aren't required, but this is the only time we'll advise you not to follow the locals – definitely wear one. Be careful on roads with tram tracks as it's easy to get your wheels stuck, and watch out for cars and pedestrians (even on designated cycle lanes). *www.gira-bicicletasdelisboa.pt*

By public transport

An umbrella organization, Transportes Metropolitanos de Lisboa (TML) incorporates the separate bodies that run the city's buses, trams and funiculars (Carris); metro (MetroLisboa); trains (CP Comboios de Portugal); ferries (TTSL); and transport to the south bank of the Tejo and its environs (Fertagus trains and TST buses). The easiest way to pay for tickets is with a rechargeable Viva Viagem card, which you can buy and top up at all train and metro stations. Locals tend to buy TML's monthly pass, which allows unlimited travel on all Lisbon and wider Lisbon transport for €40 (free for under-12s). Leave plenty of time to buy your ticket – queues can be lengthy, especially on the first day of the month, when Lisboetas line up en masse to charge their monthly pass.

By car and taxi

Narrow streets and parking shortages make getting around by car difficult, so it's only worth driving if you really must. For the same reasons, taxis can be slow and expensive. If you do want a cab, flag down a traditional taxi or use a ride-sharing app like Uber, Bolt or Free Now. Just make sure you're standing in a spot that's accessible to cars before hailing your ride.

Download these

We recommend you download these apps to help you get about the city.

WHAT3WORDS
Your geocoding friend

A what3words address is a simple way to communicate any precise location on earth, using just three words. ///encoder.values.rating, for example, is the code for the Museu do Fado. Simply download the free what3words app, type a what3words address into the search bar, and you'll know exactly where to go.

CITYMAPPER
Your journey planner

More comprehensive and easier to use than Lisbon's official public transport app (Lisboa MoveMe), Citymapper offers live info on the best routes from A to B, using trams, buses, bikes, taxis and more. There's real-time info on departures and delays, too.

Lisbon's **bairros** *(neighbourhoods) each have their own character and community. Here we take a look at some of our favourites.*

Lisbon

NEIGHBOURHOODS

Alcântara

Up until the 1990s, this was the city's docklands. Since then, former warehouses have been revamped into uber-hip bars, restaurants and co-working spaces – hello, Lx Factory and Village Underground. {map 5}

Alfama

Gentrification and mass tourism have driven up rent prices in this neighbourhood but it's still got an old-school feel. Long-time residents chat from open windows and fado drifts through the narrow streets. {map 1}

Alvalade

Cool cafés, buzzing clubs and chicken shops galore (not to mention Lisbon University's campus) make Alvalade the city's student heartland. {map 6}

Arroios

For years, Arroios was considered a no-go zone because of its troubles with drugs and prostitution. Today, locals are reclaiming this district, campaigning for a cycle path along Avenida Almirante Reis and setting up creative workshops and underground clubs. {map 6}

Avenida

Lisboetas might not live in this shopping district, but they do swing by, weaving through the tourists to grab a quick coffee at a *quiosque* or catch the film everyone's raving about. {map 3}

Avenidas Novas

It's down to work at this business district. Off the clock, locals come here to check out the latest art exhibition at Museu Calouste Gulbenkian and hang out in the museum's lush garden. {map 5}

Bairro Alto and Bica

Bars, bars and more bars. Bairro Alto and Bica are all about the good times, with beer-toting revellers spilling out of the area's many watering holes and into the streets. {map 2}

Baixa

Before 2021, the only reason Lisboetas came to Baixa was to run errands.

But the transformation of its docklands into a riverfront promenade, complete with *quiosques*, has given them reason to linger. {map 1}

Belém

When Lisboetas want to escape the city, they head to Belém for a change of scene. Yes, it has all the museums and monuments that a tourist can hope for, but it's the riverfront promenade that's won local fans. {map 5}

Benfica

For some, it's a football club, but for many Lisboetas Benfica is the gateway to Monsanto – the city's largest park. Here, locals come to stretch their legs or soak up the city views {map 5}

Cais do Sodré

Once known as the red light district, Cais is today better known for its huge food market, trendy restaurants and lively nightlife. {map 2}

Chiado

Back in the 1900s, this is where Lisbon's writers and thinkers gathered. Sure, it's

more touristy nowadays, but the city's creative crew still come here to browse the bookshops, see a play or write in the many cafés. {map 2}

Estrela

Lisboetas dream of living in this affluent area, if only to wake up near its quasi-tropical gardens. At the weekend, families and friends flock here to goggle at the swanky mansions and stroll in the Jardim da Estrela. {map 3}

Graça

Graça is a study in contrasts, where long-time, working-class residents rub shoulders with hipsters, traditional taverns neighbour trendy wine bars and old buildings are splashed with street art. {map 4}

Marvila

Once a sleepy residential neighbourhood, riverfront Marvila is now awash with craft breweries and taprooms, offbeat art galleries and cool co-working spots. {map 6}

Mouraria

Historically a multiethnic area, Mouraria has seen contentious gentrification. Despite this, it's still hard to beat for global grub and speciality grocery stores – and traditional fado spots, too. {map 1}

Parque das Nações

Built for Expo 98, Parque das Nações (aka Oriente) is now the nexus of Lisbon's tech scene. Start-ups have set up shop in its waterfront offices, while families have moved into its apartments. {map 6}

Príncipe Real

The heart of Lisbon's LGBTQ+ scene, Príncipe Real is full of welcoming nightclubs, cool cocktail bars and fashion-forward boutiques. {map 3}

Santos and Madragoa

Brunch, speciality coffee and hip co-working spaces have made Santos and Madragoa the hood of choice for Lisbon's digital nomads. {map 3}

Lisbon
ON THE MAP

Whether you're looking for your new favourite spot or want to check out what each part of Lisbon has to offer, our maps – along with handy map references throughout the book – have you covered.

ODIVELAS

IC17

PONTINHA

CARNIDE

5

IC17

BENFICA

SÃO DOMINGO DE BENFICA

IC19

ALFRAGIDE

Parque Florestal de Monsanto

CARNAXIDE

IC17

IC15

IP7

QUEIJAS

A5

AJUDA

CRUZ-QUEBRADA

ALGÉS

BELÉM

Ponte 2 de Abr

0 kilometres   1

0 miles   1

MAP 1

1

Damas

DO OPERÁRIO

Pastelaria
Alfama Doce
E

D Ulysses

E Roda Viva

A
Museu
do Fado

RUA DO TERREIRO DO TRIGO

E EAT

As Bifanas do Afonso *(p51)*
Augusto Lisboa *(p34)*
Casa do Alentejo *(p49)*
Dear Breakfast *(p34)*
O Velho Eurico *(p47)*
Pastelaria Alfama Doce *(p37)*
Pastelaria Doce Mila *(p36)*
Roda Viva *(p54)*
Tasca Kome *(p55)*

D DRINK

Banana Café *(p81)*
Café da Garagem *(p61)*
Graça do Vinho *(p71)*
Hotel Mundial's Rooftop Bar *(p77)*
Martinho da Arcada *(p63)*
Quiosque do Carmo *(p80)*
Topo *(p76)*
Ulysses *(p73)*

S SHOP

A Outra Face da Lua *(p96)*
Conserveira de Lisboa *(p89)*
Discoteca Amália *(p100)*
The Feeting Room *(p111)*
Ginjinha Sem Rival *(p91)*
Livraria Simão *(p94)*
Louie Louie *(p102)*
Luvaria Ulisses *(p108)*
Manteigaria Silva *(p88)*
Mercado da Figueira *(p91)*

Pop Closet *(p98)*
Tropical Bairro *(p98)*

A ARTS & CULTURE

African Lisbon Tour *(p118)*
Calçada *(p121)*
Cerâmica São Vicente *(p134)*
Convento do Carmo *(p116)*
Galeria Malapata *(p128)*
MUDE *(p124)*
Museu do Aljube *(p118)*
Museu do Fado *(p117)*

N NIGHTLIFE

Botequim *(p141)*
Boutique Taberna *(p142)*
Centro LGBT *(p150)*
Damas *(p145)*
Gala Gala *(p142)*
Trobadores *(p142)*

O OUTDOORS

Alfama scenic stroll *(p170)*
Avenida da Liberdade scenic
    stroll *(p169)*
Baixa scenic stroll *(p168)*
Graça scenic stroll *(p170)*
Jardim da Cerca da Graça *(p166)*
Miradouro do Recolhimento *(p173)*
Miradouro de Santa Luzia *(p172)*
The Tejo scenic stroll *(p170)*

PRAÇA DO PRÍNCIPE REAL

E Faz Frio

A Cevicheria **E**

Artroom **A**
Pavilhão Chinês **D**

E Padaria de São Roque

RUA DAS TAIPAS

RUA DOM PEDRO V

Jardim de São Pedro de Alcântara

PRÍNCIPE REAL

RUA DE SÃO MARÇAL

RUA DA ROSA

RUA SÃO PEDRO DE ALCÂNTARA

RUA NOVA DO LOUREIRO

N Loucos e Sonhadores

Primas **N**

N Friends

RUA EDUARDO COELHO

RUA DO O SÉCULO

RUA DA ACADEMIA DAS CIÊNCIAS

Valdo Gatti **E**

A Fábrica dos Chapéus **S**

TV. DA QUEIMADA

Claus Porto **S**

Bairro do Avillez **E**

RUA DA ROSA

RUA DA MISERICÓRDIA

BAIRRO ALTO

Largo Rafael Bordalo Pinheiro 30 **A**

RUA DA CRUZ DOS POIAIS

Zé dos Bois **N**

N Tasca do Chico

Side Bar **N**

Ico **S**

S

Park **D**

CALÇADA DO COMBRO

RUA DO LORETO

RUA DA ROSA

Cabaças **E**

Carpet & Snares

Manteigaria **E**

PRAÇA L. DE CAMÕES

Sea Me **E**

O

A Brasileira **E**

28 tram route scenic stroll

CHIADO

MADRAGOA

LARGO DE QUINTELA

RUA FERNANDES TOMÁS

Quiosque do **D** Adamastor

CALÇADA DA BICA PEQUENA

Fábrica Coffee Roasters **D**

By the Wine **D**

RUA DO ALECRIM

RUA A. MARIA CARDOSO

+351 **S**

Musa da Bica **D**

RUA DA BOAVISTA

BICA

R. DO ATAÍDE

A Tabacaria **D**

La Paz **S**

RUA

Lounge **N**

PRAÇA DE SÃO PAULO

RUA DE DOM LUÍS I

D Javá

Quiosque de **D** São Paulo

Sol e **D** **E** Pesca **D**

O Bom O **D** Mau e O Vilão

N

Bacchanal

RUA DA RIBEIRA NOVA

Musicbox **N**

LARGO DO CORPO SANTO

Sala de Corte **E**

PRAÇA DOM LUÍS 1

E Time Out Market

PRAÇA DUQUE DE TERCEIRA

AVENIDA 24 DE JULHO

RUA DA CINTURA DO PORTO DE LISBOA

CAIS DO SODRÉ

Estação Ferroviária de Cais do Sodré

CAIS DO SODRÉ

PRAÇA EUROPA

| 0 metres | 200 |
| 0 yards | 200 |

B. Leza **N**

N Titanic Sur Mer

MAP 2

PRAÇA DOS ESTAURADORES

2

Estação de Caminhos de Ferro do Rossio

ROSSIO (PRAÇA DOM PEDRO IV)

🄢 Ás de Espadas

LARGO DO CARMO

RUA GARRETT Livraria
🄢 Bertrand

🄔 Burel Factory

Alma 🄔

RUA IVENS

🄢 Cerâmicas
🄐 na Linha

Museu Nacional
de Arte
Contemporânea
do Chiado

🄔 Ao 26 Vegan
CORDON

RUA DO ARSENAL

AVENIDA RIBEIRA DAS NAUS

🄔 EAT

A Cevicheria *(p52)*
Alma *(p42)*
Ao 26 Vegan *(p44)*
Bairro do Avillez *(p43)*
Cabaças *(p45)*
Faz Frio *(p53)*
Manteigaria *(p36)*
Padaria de São Roque *(p39)*
Sala de Corte *(p41)*
Sea Me *(p54)*
Sol e Pesca *(p52)*
Time Out Market *(p48)*
Valdo Gatti *(p41)*

🄓 DRINK

A Brasileira *(p62)*
A Tabacaria *(p74)*
By the Wine *(p71)*
Fábrica Coffee Roasters *(p60)*
Javá *(p79)*
Musa da Bica *(p66)*
O Bom O Mau e O Vilão *(p75)*
Park *(p76)*
Pavilhão Chinês *(p72)*
Quiosque do Adamastor *(p82)*
Quiosque de São Paulo *(p82)*

🄢 SHOP

+351 *(p108)*
A Fábrica dos Chapéus *(p109)*
Ás de Espadas *(p99)*
Burel Factory *(p104)*

Carpet & Snares *(p101)*
Cerâmicas na Linha *(p106)*
Claus Porto *(p106)*
Icon *(p104)*
Livraria Bertrand *(p94)*
La Paz *(p111)*

🄐 ARTS & CULTURE

Artroom *(p131)*
Largo Rafael Bordalo Pinheiro 30 *(p122)*
Museu Nacional de Arte Contemporânea do Chiado *(p126)*

🄝 NIGHTLIFE

B.Leza *(p145)*
Bacchanal *(p140)*
Friends *(p148)*
Loucos e Sonhadores *(p140)*
Lounge *(p154)*
Musicbox *(p152)*
Primas *(p150)*
Side Bar *(p149)*
Tasca do Chico *(p144)*
Titanic Sur Mer *(p154)*
Zé dos Bois *(p144)*

🄞 OUTDOORS

28 tram route scenic stroll *(p168)*

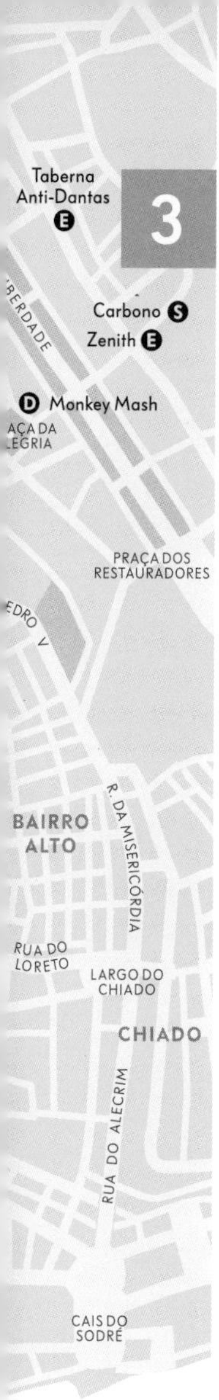

MAP 3

3

Taberna
Anti-Dantas
E

Carbono **S**
Zenith **E**

D Monkey Mash
AÇA DA
LEGRIA

'BERDADE
'DADE

PRAÇA DOS
RESTAURADORES

EDRO V

BAIRRO
ALTO

R. DA MISERICÓRDIA

RUA DO
LORETO   LARGO DO
             CHIADO

CHIADO

RUA DO ALECRIM

CAIS DO
SODRÉ

MAP 4

PRAÇA DO
ALTO DE
SÃO JOÃO

ALBUQUERQUE

DOS BARBADINHOS

Feira da Ladra

Lux Frágil

0 kilometres 1
0 miles 1

BENFICA

DAMAIA

SÃO DOMINGOS
DE BENFICA

AVENIDA LUSIADA

RADIAL DE BENFICA

IC19

ALFRAGIDE

IC17

Parque Florestal
de Monsanto ⊙

AUTOSTRADA DA COSTA DO ESTORIL

Panorâmico
de Monsanto ⊙

CAMPOLI

AVENIDA C. GULBENK

⊙
Aqueduto d
Águas Livr
scenic stro

AVE. ENGENHE

IC17

IC15

Miradouro
⊙ Keil do Amaral

Casa Pélys Ⓢ

CAMPO DE
OURIQUE

A Pad
do F

Baobá Ⓢ

AVENIDA DAS DESCOBERTAS

AVENIDA DE CEUTA

AVE INFANTE

Tapada das Necessidades ⊙

AVE DA ILHA DA MADEIRA

Gleba Ⓔ

PRAZERES

The Food For Real Ⓔ

Ⓓ Quimera
Brewpub

AJUDA

Cantina Lx ⒺⒶ Lx Factory
Ⓢ Ler Devagar

AVENI

ALCÂNTARA

Torra Ⓓ

Ⓝ Village Underground

Últ
P

Ⓞ
Pilar 7

Mosteiro dos
Jerónimos Ⓐ

BELÉM

RUA DA JUNQUEIRA

Ⓐ Cordoaria Nacional

Museu
Coleção Berardo Ⓐ

PRAÇA DO
IMPÉRIO

AVENIDA DA ÍNDIA

Ⓐ Museu de Arte,
Arquitetura e Tecnologia

Ⓐ Padrão dos
Descobrimentos

Ponte 25
de Abril

Rio Tejo

Universidade de Lisboa
5
AVENIDA DOS COMBATENTES
Casa Nepalesa
E
Fundação Calouste Gulbenkian
A
O
Jardim Gulbenkian
O
Parque Eduardo VII
PACHECO
SANTO ANTÓNIO
LARGO DO RATO
ESTRELA
DE JULHO

MAP 5

E EAT

A Padaria do Povo *(p40)*

Cantina Lx *(p51)*

Casa Nepalesa *(p42)*

The Food For Real *(p47)*

Gleba *(p38)*

Último Porto *(p53)*

D DRINK

Quimera Brewpub *(p65)*

Torra *(p63)*

S SHOP

Baobá *(p93)*

Casa Pélys *(p96)*

Ler Devagar *(p95)*

A ARTS & CULTURE

Cordoaria Nacional *(p127)*

Fundação Calouste Gulbenkian *(p126)*

Lx Factory *(p120)*

Mosteiro dos Jerónimos *(p119)*

Museu de Arte, Arquitetura e Tecnologia *(p127)*

Museu Coleção Berardo *(p124)*

Padrão dos Descobrimentos *(p116)*

N NIGHTLIFE

Village Underground *(p159)*

O OUTDOORS

Aqueduto das Águas Livres scenic stroll *(p169)*

Jardim Gulbenkian *(p167)*

Miradouro Keil do Amaral *(p172)*

Panorâmico de Monsanto *(p175)*

Parque Eduardo VII *(p165)*

Parque Florestal de Monsanto *(p165)*

Pilar 7 *(p175)*

Tapada das Necessidades *(p164)*

0 kilometres 1
0 miles 1

Aeroporto de Lisboa

AVENIDA DE BERLIM

AVENIDA INFANTE DOM HENRIQUE

OLIVAIS

AVENIDA MARECHAL GOMES DA COSTA

Jardim Mário Soares **O**

AVENIDA DO BRASIL

N RCA Club
Isco **E**   **S** A Mariazinha

A
Galeria 111

ALVALADE

AVENIDA DOS ESTADOS UNIDOS DA AMÉRICA

Universidade de Lisboa

Noir **N**
Clubbing

AVENIDA DE ROMA

AVENIDA ALMIRANTE GAGO COUTINHO

Parque de Bela Vista

AVENIDA MARECHAL ANTÓNIO DE SPINOLA

Parque Vale da Montanha

Underdogs Gallery
Bo Brewpub **D**

Fábrica Braço de Prata **N**

Oferenda **A**   **A** Fábrica
Mode

MARVILA

Lince **D**
Dois Corvos **D**

ARREEIRO

CAMPO PEQUENO

AVE JOÃO XXI

AVENIDA DA REPÚBLICA

S
Humana

AVENIDA ALMIRANTE REIS

Choupana Caffe **E**

AVENIDA DUQUE DE ÁVILA

SALDANHA

Flur **S**   **E**
Mercado de Arroios

PRAÇA DO CHILE   **A** A Avó Veio Trabalhar
Primavera **E**

RUA MORAIS SOARES

Bookshop Bivar

ARROIOS

BEATO

Drag Taste **E**

Parque Eduardo VII

Lisboa **N**
Comedy Club

Terraço Chill-Out Limão **D**

PRAÇA MARQUÊS DE POMBAL

D A.M.O. Brewery

AVENIDA ALMIRANTE REIS

N Arroz Estúdios

SANTO ANTÓNIO

AVENIDA DA LIBERDADE

Museu Nacional **A**
do Azulejo

AVE. INFANTE DOM HENRIQUE

AVENIDA INFANTE DOM HENRIQUE

GRAÇA

Ferroviário **D**

PRAÇA MARTIM MONIZ

PRAÇA DOM PEDRO IV

Rio Tejo

MAP 6

6

Parque das Nações
Ⓐ
Ⓐ Iberian Lynx

AVENIDA DOS OCEANOS

EAT

Nothing brings Lisboetas together quite like food. Eating is always a social affair, whether it's catching up over pastries, picking at a plate of petiscos or sharing a seafood feast.

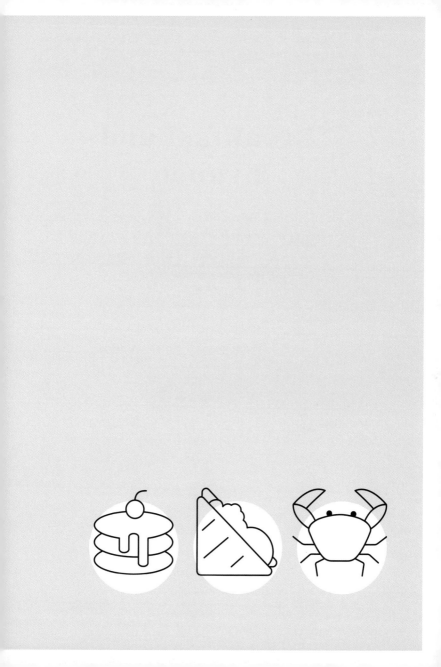

Breakfast and Brunch

An espresso and **pastel de nata** *will never get old in Lisbon, but the brunch revolution has arrived and brought with it a whole host of tasty ways to linger over the first meal of the day.*

FAUNA & FLORA

Map 3; Rua da Esperança 33, Santos and Madragoa;
///blinking.snappy.thing; www.faunafloralisboa.com

Lisbon's millennials (like so many) are all about that brunch scene, and Fauna & Flora marries the meal with another of their obsessions: house plants. Okay, the hanging baskets and tiny succulents might be fake, but the crispy bagels and avocado egg nests are the real deal.

CHOUPANA CAFFE

Map 6; Avenida da República 25A, Avenidas Novas;
///mailing.coder.wishes; 213 570 140

Desk-bound workers take the edge off early starts by grabbing something sweet from ever-reliable Choupana before clocking in at the office. The go-to order? A huge red-velvet croissant.

Not in a rush? Grab a copy of the latest indie mag at nearby bookshop Under the Cover to read as you fuel up.

Stuffed with a rich ganache and drizzled with butter-cream, this sweet treat powers them straight through till lunchtime.

MARIA LIMÃO

Map 4; Rua da Graça 127, Graça; ///revived.sleeping.alas; 926 256 292

After years of squeezing lemons beside hilly Graça's Miradouro da Senhora do Monte *(p173;* you'll still find a pop-up lemonade stand there on sunny afternoons), Mónica Santos opened up this bricks-and-mortar café around the corner. It might have lost its sweeping *miradouro* views, but Maria Limão still looks out on a quintessentially Lisbon scene: the bright yellow, 28 tram, trundling past once-grand buildings, with their plaster now peeling.

>> Don't leave without ordering a lemonade, of course, to accompany your heaped plate of pancakes.

DRAG TASTE

Map 6; Rua do Grilo 112, Marvila; ///pulsing.cleans.chain;
www.dragtaste.com

Family life is given a drag spin here. Like any good Portuguese *avó* (grandma), Pedro Pico, aka Grandma Teresa Al Dente, stuffs her guests with bacon and eggs, fruit salads and *pastéis de nata*, while rocking pearls, cat-eye glasses and the highest beehive you ever did see. Afterwards, expect a raucous post-brunch show from Grandma's extended drag family.

ZENITH

Map 3; Rua do Telhal 4A, Avenida; ///tapers.blanked.wire;
www.zenithcaffe.pt

Zenith's all-day brunch and cocktail menu fits perfectly with Lisboetas' dance-till-dawn approach to partying. Early doors, the place throngs with fresh-faced exercisers; come 2pm, bleary-eyed partiers mooch in for hair-of-the-dog mojitos and fortifying plates of pancakes.

AUGUSTO LISBOA

Map 1; Rua Santa Marinha 26, Alfama; ///earliest.stadium.worker;
962 625 552

A little hungry, mildly hungry or very hungry: that's how Augusto categorizes its brunch selection. So, if you're still pretty full from last night's slap-up dinner, order a super-healthy juice or light scrambled eggs. Ravenous? Go for a piled-high plate of avocado-and-egg toast or a hearty bowl of oatmeal – and don't skimp on dessert.

» Don't leave without trying the banana bread. It's served hot and coated in black sesame seeds and a homemade peanut sauce.

DEAR BREAKFAST

Map 1; Largo de Santo António da Sé 16, Alfama;
///announce.sailed.steaming; www.dearbreakfast.com

It's official: breakfast isn't just for breakfast any more. Here at Dear Breakfast, heaped stacks of pancakes and the obligatory avocado on toast are served up all day long, offering its late-rising Alfama regulars a relaxed place to enjoy their favourite meal at any time they like.

Liked by the locals

"Breakfast has long been neglected in Lisbon. We traditionally start the day with a strong espresso and a pastry – just enough to hold us through to lunch. But places like Dear Breakfast, with its healthy and varied menu, aim to make breakfast the best meal of the day."

NUNO PEREIRA, WAITER AT DEAR BREAKFAST

Pastelarias and Padarias

There's more to Lisbon's baking scene than pastéis
de nata (custard tarts). *On top of centuries-old bakes,
ambitious artisan carb-dealers are creating the likes of
vegan* empadas (savoury pies) *and gluten-free pastries.*

PASTELARIA DOCE MILA

Map 1; Beco dos Cavaleiros 15, Mouraria; ///seated.remote.unwell; 218 853 183

Move over *pastel de nata*, there's a new pastry in town: *pastel de Mouraria*. Like their custard cousins, these white-bean-and-almond tarts are the perfect snack to eat on the go – if you can resist lingering over a coffee in Doce Mila's sunny little courtyard, that is.

MANTEIGARIA

Map 2; Rua do Loreto 2, Bairro Alto; ///talents.renting.nitrogen; 213 471 492

The best *pastel de nata* in town? It's a hard-fought contest, but we reckon Manteigaria's bake – with its flaky yet crunchy pastry shell, and warm and gooey, cinnamon-dusted centre – is in with a good shot. While tourists make a beeline for the tile-crusted façade of Pastéis de Belém – the city's OG *pastelaria* – Lisboetas form an orderly-but-impatient queue outside Manteigaria as soon as a new batch comes out of the oven. Most locals will tell you that these *pastéis* are well-worth the wait, but we'll let you be the judge of that.

» **Don't leave without** ordering a glass of *capilé* on a hot day. This iced-tea-style drink is made with a traditional Portuguese syrup.

PASTELARIA ALFAMA DOCE

Map 1; Rua da Regueira 39, Alfama; ///moguls.dusts.field; 933 143 460

Lazy Saturday strollers meandering around Alfama's maze-like, crooked alleys make sure to stumble (accidentally on purpose) upon the door of this *pastelaria*. Part of the joy here is peeking into the pastry cabinet, loaded with sweet treats like *pastéis de nata*, *folhados de maçã* (apple turnovers) and *pastéis de Alfama* (a little-known cottage-cheese tart with a touch of almond and lemon). Add steaming cups of 50-cent coffee and it's the perfect place to refuel before getting back out into the labyrinth.

Try it!
BAKE YOUR OWN

Whip up your own batch of *pastéis de nata* by signing up for a class with the Compadre Cooking school *(www.compadrecooking.pt)*. Your homework will be to try some other Portuguese pastry recipes, too.

ISCO

Map 6; Rua José d'Esaguy 10D, Alvalade; ///hoofs.tarred.sugar;
211 345 751

Few people are willing to schlep out to Alvalade, but Nordic-style bakery ISCO is reason alone to make the trip. Paris-perfect croissants, and pillowy *kanelbullar* and *kardemummabullar* (or cinnamon and cardamom rolls to those who don't speak Swedish), have pastry devotees hopping on the metro and crossing the city on the regular.

GLEBA

Map 5; Rua Maria Pia 2–4, Alcântara; ///typhoon.refrain.moon;
www.mygleba.com

Troubled by the increasing industrialization of breadmaking, in 2016 20-year-old Diogo Amorim set out to revive traditional Portuguese recipes and methods – and shook up Lisbon's *padaria* (bakery) scene

Shh!

It's after dark and you've got a serious case of the munchies. Make your way to one of Lisbon's best-kept secrets, its late-night bakeries: Bolos Quentes in Alcântara *(www. bolos-quentes-alcantara.negocio. site)* and Fábrica dos Bolos do Chile in Arroios *(www.fabricados bolosdochile.pt)*. Doors open at 8pm and from then till 6am a steady stream of fans trickle in from the nearby clubs to grab a sweet treat or savoury bite. Go on, your rumbling tummy will thank you.

like an earthquake as a result. The whole process at Gleba is a real labour of love: Diogo uses local grains, grinds his own flour and waits for the dough to rise naturally. Come to pick up delicious sourdough loaves and buns, perfect for a picnic lunch.

PADARIA DE SÃO ROQUE

Map 2; Rua Dom Pedro V 57, Príncipe Real; ///direct.sharper.using; www.panifsroque.pt

Way back in the 1960s, the small bakeries scattered across Bairro Alto came together to form a united baking front, sharing grain, equipment and a warehouse. They were known as the *catedral do pão* (bread cathedral), a name emblazoned in *azulejos* under Padaria de São Roque's ecclesiastical-style domed ceiling. Bread is still worshipped here, but hungry pilgrims also venerate sweet treats like cookies and custard tarts.

» Don't leave without trying a *broa de Coimbra*, a sweet bread stuffed with raisins, nuts and candied fruit. Praise be!

MOKO VEGGIE CAFÉ

Map 4; Rua do Forno do Tijolo 29D, Arroios; ///muffin.blank.behave; 21 8 130 621

Renato Lai is on a quest to help sweet-toothed Lisboetas forgo milk, eggs and anything animal. And the city's fast-growing vegan community is grateful, packing out Renato's café come lunchtime. Here, they tuck into buttery-but-butter-free croissants, plant-based cakes and toasties oozing with vegan cheese.

Special Occasion

Finally submitted that project? Entering a new decade of birthdays? Despite being a relaxed bunch, Lisboetas know when an occasion demands a proper celebration and where to book a table to toast it.

GEOGRAPHIA

Map 3; Rua do Conde 1, Santos and Madragoa; ///works.thumps.lasted; www.restaurantegeographia.pt

So, it's your birthday. Make for this relaxed restaurant, just around the corner from the Museu Nacional de Arte Antiga. While the museum showcases the world's ancient art, Geographia celebrates its food. The globe-trotting menu features *feijoada* (black bean stew) from Brazil, shrimp curry from Goa and the "best sponge cake in the universe" from Portugal – an obvious birthday-party order.

A PADARIA DO POVO

Map 5; Rua Luís Derouet 20A, Campo de Ourique; ///slap.city.typist; www.apadariadopovo.weebly.com

A Padaria do Povo has a varied history. In 1919, it was the tiny Universidade Popular university. Next, it became a neighbourhood bakery, hence the name, "the people's bakery". And, now, it's a

Portuguese-Goan restaurant popular with Campo de Ourique's students, who celebrate handing in assignments over *petiscos* (the Portuguese version of tapas) and *xacuti* (a Goan curry spiced with white poppy seeds). After, they dance to the live music – when the football isn't on, that is. That's when A Padaria do Povo becomes the hottest place in town to cheer on Benfica and Sporting, Lisbon's teams.

VALDO GATTI

Map 2; Rua do Grémio Lusitano 13, Bairro Alto;
///dolphin.filled.enforced; www.valdogatti.com

There's fierce competition for the title of Lisbon's best pizzeria. But we think this neighbourhood spot edges it. Why? Because it's the most authentic slice this side of Naples. Piping hot sourdough-based pies fly out of a wood-fired oven, all topped with organic produce imported from Italy and proudly served by outgoing Italian staff bustling between tables.

>> Don't leave without toasting with a glass of organic local wine. This place has one of the best lists of small-batch producers in the city.

SALA DE CORTE

Map 2; Praça Dom Luís I 7, Cais do Sodré; ///brings.otters.control;
www.saladecorte.pt

The ultimate date-night dish? It's got to be steak, and nowhere in Lisbon does it better than Sala de Corte. Here, T-bones, entrecôte and the like are cooked over charcoal in a Josper oven, making them super tender. Go on, splash out and share one of the bigger cuts.

ALMA

Map 2; Rua Anchieta 15, Chiado; ///officer.flap.delivers; www.almalisboa.pt

Good ol'-fashioned Portuguese cooking gets a chic new makeover at this date-night staple (yes, it has two Michelin stars). Here, cuddled-up couples share celebrity chef Henrique Sá Pessoa's "Costa a Costa" menu, a parade of seafood dishes from the local coast, or the "Alma", a fusion of Portuguese and Asian flavours. Reservations are a must.

CASA NEPALESA

Map 5; Avenida Elias Garcia 172A, Avenidas Novas; ///fillers.reap.puddles; www.casanepalesa.pt

Thanks to Lisbon's growing Nepalese community, you're never too far away from a tasty *momo* (stuffed dumpling). Chef Tanka Sapkota has elevated humble Nepalese homecooking into a fine-dining art,

Shh!

Keep your eyes peeled for any red Chinese lanterns hanging from apartment windows in Mouraria and Martim Moniz. They often signify a *"clandestino"* – the unregulated Chinese restaurants popular with students and savvy locals looking for a wallet-friendly feast to fuel their nights out. Next time you want to celebrate delivering a big project (or just making it through the working week), gather the gang and head out into the streets, looking for a glowing globe.

but without the price tag. In Casa Nepalesa's dark and intense interior, he serves up soups that have been simmered with hand-ground spices for hours, heaped bowls of rice fed by Himalayan water and curries made with the very best Portuguese meat (think Transmontano goatling, Alentejan lamb and wild boar from Évora). And the *momos*? They're stuffed with acorn-fed, black Alentejan pork and free-range chicken, and washed down with Portuguese wine. If you're new to Nepalese, you can count on the friendly waiters to help you assemble the perfect festive meal.

BAIRRO DO AVILLEZ

Map 2; Rua Nova da Trindade 18, Baixa; ///bitters.bright.speeding; www.bairrodoavillez.pt

Cascais-born chef José Avillez has been on a one-man mission to raise the profile of Portuguese gastronomy, and with two Michelin stars to his name, he's more than succeeded. Now he's added this upscale food court, featuring four individual concessions, to his roster of restaurants. Páteo, which occupies the airy, plant-filled atrium, is all about seafood; Taberna, by the entrance, serves up charcuterie and cheese boards; Mini Bar offers cocktails, live music and a swanky tasting menu; and Pizzaria Lisboa, well, we don't need to tell you what'll you'll find here. It's a great place to spend the evening with a group of friends, toasting promotions, birthdays or just the impending weekend.

» Don't leave without ordering the grilled blue lobster if it's on Páteo's constantly changing menu. The buttery sauce it's slathered in will blow your mind (and your wallet).

Comfort Food

A late, lazy dinner is the Lisbon way. In Europe's mildest city, comfort food is all about lingering over a meal with your nearest and dearest. And when the food is this good, you won't want to rush it.

AO 26 VEGAN

Map 2; Rua Vítor Cordon 26, Chiado; ///soils.quintet.blanket; www.ao26vegan.eatbu.com

Portuguese staples are very meat-heavy, but you don't need to miss out if you're all about that plant-based diet. The inventive chefs at Ao 26 have given comforting Portuguese classics the vegan treatment, with fried mushroom replacing the usual cuttlefish in its *choco frito* and seitan stepping in for pork in the *bifana* sandwich.

PRIMAVERA

Map 6; Rua Morais Soares 101, Arroios; ///learning.debating.little; 218 149 804

When you want to call someone an expert in Portugal, you say *"são muitos anos a virar frangos"* (they've been turning chickens for many years). And, with over half a century at the spit, this place is the literal embodiment of the phrase. But don't just take

Prefer your chicken with a spicy kick? Make sure to ask for lashings of the house piri-piri sauce.

our word for it: come hungry to enjoy charcoal-grilled chicken served the Portuguese way (yes, that's with both fries and rice).

CABAÇAS

Map 2; Rua das Gáveas 8, Bairro Alto; ///talents.coconut.stressed; 213 463 443

Bringing a whole new meaning to the term "home-cooking", Cabaças is a DIY restaurant where diners become chefs, sizzling their own steak on the stone right at the table. It's a popular experience, with groups happily waiting up to an hour for the privilege. Leave your name at the door and hop into a Bairro Alto bar while you wait.

KERALA

Map 4; Rua Passos Manuel 14, Arroios; ///dramatic.shared.shutting; 968 463 303

Feeling homesick for the spicy, aromatic flavours they grew up with, husband-and-wife team Vijeesh and Thrinisha Rajan opened this Keralan restaurant. Here, heartwarming south Indian dishes (*masala dosas*, chutneys, curries) inspired by family recipes are accompanied by travel tips for Vijeesh and Thrinisha's beloved home state. Come for a long-awaited catch-up and linger over the family-style sharing plates.

» Don't leave without tucking into a scoop of the heavenly rose petal ice cream. Legend has it that Vijeesh first made it for his wife to apologise after an argument. We bet she forgave him in a flash.

Solo, Pair, Crowd

Whether it's a table for one or a feast with the whole squad, this city has got your cravings covered.

FLYING SOLO

Working hard or hardly working

Lisbon's ever-growing community of digital nomads are big fans of farm-to-table concept Maria Food Hub, fuelling their days with bowls of eggs and stacked burgers.

IN A PAIR

Late-night date

Drinks turned into dinner? Impress your date by topping off an evening out in Bairro Alto with Brazilian street food at Acarajé da Carol. Owner Carol is the perfect host, keeping your plates piled high and fruity cocktails topped up.

FOR A CROWD

Sharing is caring

We can't predict what's cooking at community kitchen Zona Franca dos Anjos. One day you could be eating falafel, the next Cape Verdean *cachupa*. But you can bet on it being delicious — and often accompanied by board games and jam sessions.

THE FOOD FOR REAL

Map 5; Rua dos Lusíadas 51A, Alcântara; ///quarrel.punt.matrons;
www.thefoodforreal.com

Comfort food often means carbs, which can be a raw deal for coeliacs. The Food For Real is working hard to change that with its 100 per cent gluten-free menu. Alcântara's creatives love it, settling in for leisurely "working lunches" over pillowy scones and tapioca pancakes.

TAMBARINA

Map 3; Rua do Poço dos Negros 94, Santos and Madragoa;
///joins.delved.fades; 967 181 400

Picture this: a no-frills, blue-white-and-red dining room, musicians playing peppy, Funaná tracks and heaped plates of *cachupa* (a slow-cooked stew made with corn, beans, sweet potato and meat). No, you haven't been transported to Praia – this is Tambarina, Lisbon's best Cape Verdean restaurant.

» Don't leave without trying the homemade punch. Choose coconut, tamarind or the pure – and potent – Cape Verdean grog.

O VELHO EURICO

Map 1; Largo São Cristóvão 4, Mouraria; ///plug.mixer.dished;
218 861 815

Tascas (taverns) are all about sharing good food with good friends. And O Velho Eurico is no different. Here, Mouraria families and out-of-towners (often escorted by their Portuguese hosts) dissect their days over tasty, traditional dishes like lamb croquettes and duck rice.

Light Bites

Small plates are big in Lisbon – in more ways than one. Sandwiches are stuffed with fillings and evenings always kick off with plates upon plates of petiscos *(Portugal's bigger and better version of tapas).*

TIME OUT MARKET

Map 2; Avenida 24 de Julho, Cais do Sodré; ///hardens.stumble.copy;
www.timeoutmarket.com/lisboa

We'd be mad not to feature this place, even if its reputation is down to its international fans rather than Lisboetas. Come with friends to graze on sushi and *pastéis de bacalhau* (cod cakes) from the 40-something off shoots of Lisbon's top restaurants (according to Time Out, that is).

» Don't leave without checking out the Time Out Studio upstairs. It hosts everything from intimate concerts to wine tastings.

MERCADO DE ARROIOS

Map 6; Rua Ângela Pinto, Arroios; ///rots.emerald.quit

Move over the Time Out Market: it's all about the Mercado de Arroios now. It might be smaller than its more famous cousin, but Mercado de Arroios still presents an array of foodie treats to choose from. Senior Lisboetas enjoy sandwiches from Terrapão bakery, creatives on their (long) lunch breaks tuck into *petiscos* from Tasca do Mercado and students share mezze from Mezze (go figure). The latter is Lisbon's first Syrian restaurant, staffed entirely by refugees and co-founded by Alaa Alhariri – an architecture student who was missing her country's bread.

CASA DO ALENTEJO

Map 1; Rua Portas de Santo Antão 58, Baixa; ///tanked.allows.them; www.casadoalentejo.pt

So, you've heard of the Algarve, but what about the Alentejo? This oft-ignored Portuguese region gets far fewer visitors than its package-holidayed-out southern neighbour. Tucked down an alley, Casa do Alentejo is a celebration of all the region has to offer. In the intricately tiled, riad-style courtyard, groups of girlfriends dig into plates of Alentejan olives, cheese and other *petiscos*, and glug from jugs of Alentejan wine, while listening to Alentejan music.

Try it!
JOIN A CLASS

As well as housing a restaurant, Casa do Alentejo is a cultural centre, promoting Alentejan gastronomy, music, literature and culture. Sign up for a cooking lesson or dance class to learn more about this region.

Liked by the locals

"Portuguese *petiscos* are often compared to Spanish tapas, but really the only similarity is the sense of conviviality. Any occasion, and any hour, is an appropriate time to *petiscar* with friends."

DANIEL COELHO, TOUR GUIDE WITH BIKE MY SIDE SIDECAR TOURS

AS BIFANAS DO AFONSO

Map 1; Rua da Madalena 146, Baixa; ///goodbye.premises.starting

Come lunchtime, Baixa workers have only one thing in mind: a *bifana*. And this place makes the best. Thick slices of pork simmer away in garlic and white wine before being slid into a too-small bun. (Okay, we might be pushing "light bites" a bit here.)

O GAMBUZINO

Map 4; Rua dos Anjos 5A, Arroios; ///bench.social.smaller;
www.ogambuzino.com

O Gambuzino's sticky cauliflower bites and citrusy mushroom "scallops" come with a complimentary feel-good glow. Why? This plant-based spot has teamed up with Fruta Feia, a local cooperative that rescues fruit and veg rejected by supermarkets for not meeting their standards. Imperfect food made perfect, or so the locals say.

» Don't leave without ordering a glass of *kombucha* (homebrewed fermented tea). It's an acquired taste.

CANTINA LX

Map 5; Lx Factory, Rua Rodrigues Faria 103, Alcântara;
///rescuer.tube.lizard; www.cantinalx.com

Way back when super-hip Lx Factory was still a working factory, this canteen dished out hearty lunches to the illustrious staff. Today, Cantina serves lighter bites – think soups, charcuterie and cheese-boards – to the area's artsy office workers come lunchtime.

Seafood Spots

Are there really 365 different ways to cook bacalhau*?*
This legend could well be true, with Lisbon's
chefs setting the seafood scene alight with
their inventive dishes.

A CEVICHERIA

Map 2; Rua Dom Pedro V 129, Príncipe Real; ///impaired.assure.forget;
www.acevicheria.pt

A year's worth of seafood recipes? And even more when you fuse
Portuguese dishes with the very best of South American cooking,
which is exactly what chef Francisco "Kiko" Martins is doing in this
playful space. Beneath the swirling tentacles of an enormous fake
octopus (yes, really), dapper young couples pick at ceviche platters
and sip pisco sours.

SOL E PESCA

Map 2; Rua Nova do Carvalho 44, Cais do Sodré; ///spit.opposite.defend;
213 467 203

Forget what you think you know about canned goods: in Portugal,
tinned fish doesn't just collect dust at the back of kitchen cupboards,
it's practically a food group. Gain a greater appreciation of canned

seafood at Sol e Pesca, a former tackle shop crammed with fishing nets, lobster pots and stack upon stack of colourful tins. Take your pick from the menu, which comes attached to a fishing rod, and the chef will whip up something delicious (like a refreshing salad topped with tinned octopus or sharing plates of spicy sardine *petiscos*).

» Don't leave without picking up some cans to take home. You're bound to have a new love for tinned tuna after eating here.

FAZ FRIO

Map 2; Rua Dom Pedro V 96, Príncipe Real; ///punks.tablet.bombard; www.fazfrio.pt

One of the longest-running seafood restaurants in town, this centuries-old *taberna* has been the site of conspiracies, literary gatherings and sailor meet-ups over the years. Today, it's all about loud celebrations with friends rather than clandestine conversations in corners. But, just like in the old days, codfish still takes centre stage here, albeit with a contemporary spin. Add the codfish fritters with turnip and rice to your list of *bacalhau* recipes.

ÚLTIMO PORTO

Map 5; Estação Marítima da Rocha do Conde de Óbidos, Alcântara; ///pocket.surfed.standing; 213 979 498

As great as the city's restaurants are, you can't beat eating seafood with the scent of the sea in the air and the sound of water lapping nearby. At this lunch spot set on the docks, the catch of the day is flung up and grilled immediately on hot coals. You can't get fresher than that.

SEA ME

Map 2; Rua do Loreto 21, Chiado; ///votes.teachers.wipe;
www.peixariamoderna.com

Lisbon may be full of seafood restaurants, but fishmongers are a dying breed. Sea Me wants to change that by modernizing the concept of a fish shop. Long-time locals still buy Atlantic-caught fish by the kilo here (at market prices, naturally), but a younger crew come to savour Portuguese-style sushi (think sardine nigiri and black squid tempura).

RODA VIVA

Map 1; Beco do Mexias 11 R/c, Alfama; ///nuggets.trains.craters;
218 871 730

Fado is replaced by African beats at Roda Viva, everyone's favourite Mozambican restaurant. Bringing an East African spin to the local catch, chef Octávio Chamba serves up scrumptious shrimp *matapa* (a warm and fuzzy stew made with fresh greens and fragrant peanuts) to his devoted fans.

» **Don't leave without** accompanying your *matapa* with a bottle of Laurentina, Mozambique's signature beer.

CERVEJARIA RAMIRO

Map 4; Avenida Almirante Reis 1-H, Arroios; ///readily.airbag.unravel;
www.cervejariaramiro.com

Arroios families had been coming to Ramiro long before celebrity chef Anthony Bourdain rolled up in 2012 and let the secret out to the rest of the world. And the rest of the world certainly seems to be

To skip the queue, book a table for 7pm. Yes it's a very un-Lisbon hour, but think of the food.

happily standing in line outside, peeking through the door to see lucky diners clinking glasses and cracking open crab and lobster shells.

TASCA KOME

Map 1; Rua da Madalena 57, Baixa; ///cats.backers.envy; 211 340 117

Lisbon and the Japanese city of Osaka are surprisingly similar. Both revolve around the great rivers that slice through them (the Tejo and Yodo), both have been devastated by earthquakes (1755 and 2018) and both are seafood-obsessed. Cementing the similarities even more is this street food spot, a hit with Japanese families who trek here from Cascais on the regular for *takoyaki* (chewy octopus, tempura scraps and pickled ginger encased in a perfectly crisp batter that bursts open in the mouth).

TABERNA ANTI-DANTAS

Map 3; Rua de São José 196, Baixa; ///rugs.clock.emperor;
www.valisedimage.wixsite.com/taberna-antidantasen

Never heard of *Anti-Dantas*? Let us fill you in – it's an influential counter-cultural manifesto written by artist José de Almada Negreiros in 1915, which defended the avant-garde movement and attacked the critics, like Júlio Dantas, who tried to halt its creativity. Decorated with pages from this modernist declaration, this similarly creative *taberna* shakes up traditional Portuguese cooking, hiding fish soup within a crusty bread roll and filling *pastéis de nata* with cod.

A foodie afternoon in
Campo de Ourique

Campo de Ourique's transformation from a sleepy suburb to a gourmet hub started in 2013, when trendy food stalls popped up in its market (a whole year before the headline-hogging Time Out Market). Here, young entrepreneurs fill vegan tacos beside long-time market traders hawking fruit and veg. Spend the afternoon hopping between the market and surrounding restaurants, cafés and *pastelarias* to experience the traditional and innovative sides of Lisbon's foodie scene.

1. Café da Gema
Rua Coelho da Rocha 130, Campo de Ourique; 214 046 272
///detained.intelligible.grass

2. Mercado de Campo de Ourique
Rua Coelho da Rocha 104, Campo de Ourique; 211 323 701
///mini.quicker.dumpy

3. Vegan Nata
Rua 4 de Infantaria 29B, Campo de Ourique;
www.vegannata.pt
///smallest.sung.heat

4. Pigmeu
Rua 4 de Infantaria 68, Campo de Ourique;
www.pigmeu.pt
///visitors.together.areas

Pop into
CAFÉ DA GEMA

Feeling a bit tired? Fuel up with a *maté* (a caffeine-rich Brazilian tea) and *coxinhas* (teardrop-shaped croquettes stuffed with chicken) at Café da Gema.

 Jardim da Parada ///soft.chicken.title

RUA DE CAMPO DE OURIQUE

Dig in at
PIGMEU

Locals rave about this
farm-to-table restaurant,
which specializes in pork
dishes. Order a *bifana* to
see what all the fuss is about.

4

RUA TOMÁS DA ANUNCIAÇÃO

RUA FRANCISCO METRASS

CORREIA TELES

RUA AZEDO GNECO

CAMPO DE OURIQUE

SANTA ISABEL

RUA SILVA CARVALHO

3

Treat yourself at
VEGAN NATA

Vegans rejoice: this pint-size
bakery serves up butter- and
egg-free *pastéis de nata*. Order
at the counter and devour your
pastel while it's still warm.

RUA DO 4 DE INFANTARIA

RUA FERREIRA BORGES

The **Jardim da Parada**
*is a pleasant leafy spot
to take a break – though
there's a kiosk flipping
burgers here if you're
still hungry.*

A COELHO DA ROCHA

2

Peruse the stands at the
MERCADO DE CAMPO
DE OURIQUE

Stock up on canned sardines,
jams and other scrumptious
staples at Campo de Ourique's
market. Ravenous? Pick up a
petisco or two while you browse.

RUA SARAIVA DE CARVALHO

A SARAIVA DE CARVALHO

0 metres	150
0 yards	150

DRINK

Thanks to Lisbon's 300 days of sunshine a year, locals spend a lot of their free time drinking alfresco. Seek out the city's unique quiosques (kiosks) or stake out a rooftop bar.

Coffee Shops

Forget Italian espresso. Lisbon's bica *is bigger,
better and smoother – or so the locals say.
(And don't get them started on the differences
between a* galão *and a latte.)*

FÁBRICA COFFEE ROASTERS

**Map 2; Rua das Flores 63, Chiado; ///shorter.hydrant.navigate;
www.fabricacoffeeroasters.com**

Fábrica brought the global coffee revolution to Portugal's doorstep.
Before this pioneer hit the scene in 2015, Lisbon's coffee shops were
pit stops, where locals downed *bicas* espresso-style before swiftly
hitting the road. Fábrica changed all that with its frothy cappuccinos,
picture-perfect lattes and drip coffees, all made to be savoured.

BUNA

**Map 3; Rua do Poço dos Negros 168, Santos and Madragoa;
///quantity.dirt.altering; 910 997 193**

Remote workers and coffee shops: they just go together. And
Lisbon's ever-growing community of digital nomads can't get
enough of Buna. It's quiet (apart from the tapping of other laptop-
users), has strong and stable WiFi, and serves up the best Nitro

Walk over to Flor da Selva, one of the city's oldest roasters, to learn how beans turn into coffee.

cold brew coffee in the city. Need some sustenance? Buna's got you there, too. The oozing toasties and homemade cakes will help you power through your work.

CAFÉ DA GARAGEM

Map 1; Costa do Castelo 75, Mouraria; ///smelter.sweat.pressing; www.teatrodagaragem.com

Perhaps the perfect accompaniment to a coffee isn't a pastry, but a view. It certainly seems that way at Café da Garagem, where you'll quickly discover that the guidebooks weren't exaggerating about *"a luz de Lisboa"* – the enchanting golden light that seems to always shine on this beautiful city. Order an afternoon *galão* (the café isn't open in the morning), settle into one of the comfy armchairs by the floor-to-ceiling windows and soak up the postcard-pretty scenes of Alfama's red roofs and white façades tumbling down the hill.

» Don't leave without making plans to return in the evening, when the café hosts jazz concerts, poetry recitals and sunset scenes.

LE PETIT PRINCE

Map 3, Rua Cecílio de Sousa 1A, Príncipe Real; ///cabbage.probable.mincing; 213 471 607

With its tiny tables, crumbling plaster and abstract wall art, Le Petit Prince seems to have been plucked from a backstreet of Paris. Here, girlfriends cradle matcha lattes, tuck into fluffy croissants and brush up on their French by raiding the bookshelves.

CURVA

Map 4; Rua Damasceno Monteiro 108D, Graça;
///younger.packages.scared; 939 024 924

Curva takes its art seriously. No, we're not talking about latte art (although the baristas top every cup with a flawless heart). This coffeehouse supports local artists by exhibiting and selling their work in the gallery out back. No wonder creatives flock here for inspiration and a much-needed caffeine hit.

A BRASILEIRA

Map 2; Rua Garrett 122, Chiado; ///swimmer.shiver.hooks;
www.abrasileira.pt

When it first opened in 1905, A Brasileira quickly became a favourite meeting point for the city's intellectuals, artists and writers. Among them was Fernando Pessoa, the enigmatic Portuguese poet, who enjoyed sitting in this café with a *bica* while he smoked, read

Shh!

Unless they're planning to redecorate their homes, locals are unlikely to pop into Marquise *(Rua Nova da Piedade 33)*. But if they did, they'd discover that this home decor store has a little-known café hidden within it. Those who've been let in on the secret stake out its vine-shaded courtyard, where they sip speciality coffee and snack on the likes of Turkish eggs and Lebanese *kibbeh* (meatballs).

and wrote. Today, students from the Universidade de Lisboa's nearby faculty of fine arts gather here after class, side-stepping the inevitable hordes of photo-snapping tourists as they make their way to their favourite table. Why come to such a touristy spot, you may ask? Perhaps they're hoping that Pessoa's talents will rub off on them, ahead of their next essay submission.

» Don't leave without checking out the life-size bronze statue of the man himself, Fernando Pessoa, who sits at a table outside.

TORRA
Map 5; Travessa do Conde da Ponte 1, Alcântara; ///gadgets.episode.grew; www.torra.pt

There are no barriers to good coffee at Torra. Literally: there's no counter standing between the caffeine-obsessed crowd and the baristas here. Torra is all about bringing coffee to the people, with the staff freely demonstrating how to make a mean brew, selling aeropress kits, dripper tools and bags of beans, and running latte art workshops. Sign us up.

MARTINHO DA ARCADA
Map 1; Praça do Comércio 3, Baixa; ///navigate.aimless.those; www.martinhodaarcada.pt

Since it first opened its doors in 1782, Martinho da Arcada has fuelled fado divas and Nobel prize-winners. Whispers: okay, the coffee here is average, and, yes, the food is a little overpriced. But sipping your morning *galão* alongside a sizeable slice of local history? Priceless.

Craft Breweries

Under Salazar's regime, Lisboetas could only drink the two national lagers: Sagres or Super Bock. Fortunately for beer-lovers, those days are long gone and the beer scene is burgeoning with all kinds of crafts.

DOIS CORVOS

Map 6; Rua Capitão Leitão 94, Marvila;
///included.tumble.coherent; www.doiscorvos.pt

After living in beer-mad Seattle, Susana Cascais and Scott Steffens were shocked at Lisbon's non-existent craft scene when they moved here in 2013. Enter Dois Corvos, the brewery that spurred Marvila's transformation from a long-neglected neighbourhood into a cool craft beer hub. Here, breweries club together to buy grains, hops and yeast, create new recipes and host events promoting Marvila-brewed beer.

BO BREWPUB

Map 6; Rua Vale Formoso 9, Marvila; ///swaps.tenses.steered;
www.cervejabolina.pt

Many an afternoon is spent whiling away the hours here, soaking up the rays and industrial views, and sipping on brews from Bolina (the craft brewery that opened the joint in 2020). A few drinks down, taking part in the Thursday pub quiz or monthly karaoke night always seems an excellent idea – hey, no one was in a hurry to leave anyway, right?

QUIMERA BREWPUB

Map 5; Rua Prior do Crato 6, Alcântara; ///reversed.alcove.caravan; www.quimerabrewpub.com

Set in a stone-walled and window-less carriage tunnel, Quimera oozes cosy vibes. Plonk yourself down at a low-slung, candlelit table and find yourself among a merry mishmash of students, after-work groups and Alcântara regulars sipping too-full *imperials* (only tourists order pints). Settle in for the long haul; you won't want to miss whoever's tickling the piano keys tonight.

» Don't leave without ordering a Reuben. This deli-style toasted sandwich, oozing with Portuguese pastrami, cheese, sauerkraut and Thousand Island sauce, is a crowd-pleaser.

LINCE

Map 6; Rua Capitão Leitão 1B, Marvila; ///fewest.fear.chained; www.cervejalince.pt

Wild cats and beer might sound like a strange combo, but hear us out. For every banana-tinged Weiss, citrusy Belgian pale ale or creamy stout sold, Lince's owners António and Pedro give a percentage of the profits to a charity that protects the *lince Ibérico*, the endangered Iberian lynx. A beer that supports a good cause? Pour us a glass.

OITAVA COLINA TAPROOM

Map 4; Rua Damasceno Monteiro 8A, Graça;
///rubble.perky.dampen; www.oitavacolina.pt

Brothers Sérgio and Pedro Romão started brewing IPAs in their garage for friends and neighbours, who would happily stand in the street outside to drink their beers. As word got out about Oitava Colina and the street became chocker, the Romãos were forced to open first this taproom, then a gastropub, to meet demand. In 2021, they moved their brewery into even bigger premises in Cabo Ruivo, but the Romãos haven't forgotten their humble roots – many of the beers are named after small *vilas* (literally villages) in the Graça neighbourhood.

MUSA DA BICA

Map 2; Calçada Salvador Correia de Sá 2, Cais do Sodré;
///campers.flux.farmed; www.cervejamusa.com

The most lively of Lisbon's craft breweries, Bica is all about having a good time, rather than a quick drink. Laidback 9-to-5ers settle in for the long-haul in the brewery's lilac-hued Cais do Sodré taproom, nodding along to the peppy soundtrack and catching up on their days over bottles of beer.

A.M.O. BREWERY

Map 6; Rua Bernardim Ribeiro 53, Arroios; ///fired.limbs.lorry;
www.amobrewery.com

Microbrewery A.M.O. is a real favourite. And, by the way, when we say micro, we mean micro. A.M.O. is so tiny that most people end up drinking on the street outside, which is hardly a problem in one of Europe's sunniest cities. Grab a bottle from the indoor bar and embrace the beer-fuelled revelry as you squeeze onto the end of the communal tables, which sit under shady parasols. You'll get chatting with your neighbours in no time.

» Don't leave without ordering Amora (a refreshing saison with hints of lemon and blackberry). It's just the thing to cool you down on one of Lisbon's steamy summer days.

21 GALLAS

Map 4; Rua Angelina Vidal 53A, Graça; ///area.lawful.archives; www.gallas.beer

Newsflash: you can be serious about craft beer and still have fun with it. And that's exactly what this quirky Graça brewery brings to the scene. Look out for fruity IPAs with hints of mango, passion fruit, coffee and piri-piri (watch out for that last one – it's got quite a kick); merch proclaiming "my blood type is IPA+"; and resident short-legged pooch Bóris, who dishes out free cuddles when a brew just won't do it.

Try it!
BREW YOUR OWN

Ever wonder how to make beer? Learn from the masters at a workshop at Oficina da Cerveja *(www.oficinadacerveja.pt)*, where many of Lisbon's brewers first learned their craft. They also sell home-brewing kits.

Wine Bars

After work, Lisboetas head straight for their nearest wine bar. Here, they linger over a carafe of wine, nibble their way through plates of petiscos and catch up on the news of the day.

VINO VERO

Map 4; Travessa do Monte 30, Graça; ///sympathy.pizzas.curiosity;
www.vinovero.wine

The city's first dedicated natural wine bar, Vino Vero is the perfect introduction to organic farming and low-intervention winemaking techniques. If you don't have a clue what that means, the Italian

Shh!

You'll have to be in the right place at the right time to catch the elusive Wine with a View (*www.winewithaview.pt*). This repurposed 1960s motor tricycle travels around Lisbon, selling Portuguese wines by the glass from its hatch. Usual stops include the park near the Torre de Belém and the slopes of the Castelo São Jorge, so keep your eyes peeled as you wander around Lisbon's most picturesque spots.

owners will happily help you choose what glass to order, filling you in on processes, flavours and notes. Your chosen glass of wine is then paired with tasty *cicchetti* (the Italian version of *petiscos*), like swordfish skewers or burrata and tomato salad. *Buon appetito!*

BLACK SHEEP

Map 3; Praça das Flores 62, Príncipe Real; ///emails.sampled.rang; www.blacksheeplisboa.com

Welcome to the smallest wine bar in town: Black Sheep only has 20 bar stools, arranged around the counter. The space might be small, but the wine list is huge – there are at least 100 different bottles to try, with a focus on organic and natural wines. Sound overwhelming? Don't worry: the Brazilian owners often hang out with the producers themselves, so they'll happily fill you in on what makes each wine special and help you pick a glass.

SENHOR UVA

Map 3; Rua de Santo Amaro 66A, Estrela; ///rang.shaves.perfect; www.senhoruva.com

Wine tends to be accompanied by meaty dishes in Portugal, but not so at Senhor Uva. Here, glasses of natural wine are served alongside seasonal, plant-based *petiscos*, like green jackfruit ceviche, miso mushrooms and carrot hummus.

» Don't leave without popping across the street to sister wine and grocery store Senhor Manuel. Grab a bottle and some veggie snacks, and you're all set for a picnic in the nearby Jardim da Estrela.

Solo, Pair, Crowd

Sipping solo? On a friend date? Out with your crew? There's a wine bar for every kind of party in Lisbon.

FLYING SOLO

The glass that cheers

On Lisbon's rare cold evenings, you can't beat sitting in the comfy rocking chair by Loucos de Lisboa's fireplace with a glass of port and a good book. Bliss!

IN A PAIR

The perfect catch-up venue

Jobim is made for those long-awaited get-togethers with your BFF. The interior is always buzzing, the Brazilian-style *petiscos* are perfect for sharing and the wine list is just long enough that you won't waste any precious catch-up time looking at the menu.

FOR A CROWD

Take your pick

With a group of friends that can never agree on which bottle to order? Hit up self-service wine bar Portugal Tasting Room. On arrival, you're all equipped with a preloaded "wine card", which fills glasses at the touch of a button.

GRAÇA DO VINHO

**Map 1; Calçada da Graça 10A, Graça; ///star.bundles.tractor;
www.gracadovinho.com**

Standing behind the old pharmacy counter, the staff at Graça do
Vinho dispense Portuguese wines with as much knowledge and
care as their forebears did medicines. Today's fortifying elixirs are
accompanied by cheese platters, sausage boards and plates of
oysters. Sounds like just what the doctor ordered.

» Don't leave without trying a glass of *vinho verde*, a light, lower-
ABV and slightly sparkling wine unique to Portugal.

BY THE WINE

**Map 2; Rua das Flores, 41/43, Chiado; ///sailing.insiders.spotty;
www.bythewine.pt**

Don't know your *vinho verde* from your *vinho tinto*? No bother. The
friendly staff at this off-shoot of the Alentejan winery José Maria da
Fonseca will guide you through the taste profiles of each vintage,
and suggest *petisco* pairings for each glass.

O PIF

**Map 4; Rua Maria 43A, Arroios; ///pulp.informs.bunch;
www.opiflisboa.com**

Few locals actually ride the 28 tram – it's a sardine can of tourists and
pick-pockets – but watching this yellow, vintage icon go by never gets
old. And there's no better place to tram-spot than O Pif's terrace, with a
refreshing glass of Lisbon-grown rosé, or a white from Setúbal, in hand.

Cocktail Joints

*The city's cocktail scene has never been hotter,
thanks to imaginative mixologists who are stirring
things up – literally. Taste their creations at one of
Lisbon's storied gin bars or stylish speakeasies.*

PAVILHÃO CHINÊS

Map 2; Rua Dom Pedro V 89, Príncipe Real; ///begins.youth.cookies; 213 424 729

Luís Pinto Coelho is the man behind many of Lisbon's cocktail bars and, alongside mixology, he has a passion for antiques. After amassing a vast collection, Luís decided to show them off (or maybe he just ran out of space to store them). Enter Pavilhão Chinês, where ceramics, taxidermy and toys peer down at a well-heeled crowd nursing a delicious cocktail or two.

FOXTROT

Map 3; Travessa Santa Teresa 28, Príncipe Real; ///surprise.things.inflame; www.barfoxtrot.pt

The golden era of cocktail making? It's got to be the 1920s, when underground mixologists created potent potions for desperate drinkers in Prohibition America. And this Coelho throwback (that's right, he owns this one, too) channels the roaring 20s – you even have to ring the bell to enter. Once inside, dressed-up dates are treated to jazz tunes and classic concoctions with a twist, like the smoked negroni and spiced margarita.

MONKEY MASH

Map 3; Praça da Alegria 66B, Avenida; ///debit.shrimp.promotes; www.monkeymash.pt

Finally, a bar that Luís Pinto Coelho doesn't own. Monkey Mash is the brainchild of former bartenders Paulo Gomes and Emanuel Minez. It's housed in an old strip club, but you wouldn't know to look at it: the dark and dim confines have been transformed into a vibrant space, with colourful murals, bright yellow and blue furniture, and tropical cocktails (mezcal and sugar cane rum are key players on the menu).

» **Don't leave without** checking out Red Frog, the duo's award-winning speakeasy, which – thanks to COVID-19 closing its premises – now occupies a small space within its more flamboyant sister bar.

ULYSSES

Map 1; Rua da Regueira 16A, Alfama; ///mouse.briefer.musical; www.ulysses-lisbon-speakeasy.business.site

With its labyrinthine streets and lack of signage, Alfama is the perfect place for a speakeasy. It's finding Ulysses' door that's tricky, rather than getting through it (no passwords here). With only 12 stools, it might be small inside but it's big on bourbon, with over 60 different bottles forming the basis for its bespoke cocktails.

MATIZ POMBALINA

Map 3; Rua das Trinas 25, Santos and Madragoa; ///flannel.safely.bind;
www.matiz-pombalina.pt

Named after the Marquis de Pombal, the man who rebuilt Lisbon
after the 1755 earthquake, this bar encapsulates the style and spirit
of the Pombaline age. While partiers stand in line outside Santos
and Madragoa's high-octane clubs, a sedate crowd slinks past
them to Matiz Pombalina's *azulejo*-stamped façade. Here, they
settle into the plush 18th-century armchairs and savour gin-based
cocktails, flavoured with things like rose syrup and dried apple.

CINCO LOUNGE

Map 3; Rua Ruben A Leitão 17A, Príncipe Real; ///javelin.snoring.free;
www.cincolounge.com

This is classic date territory: candlelit tables, low, plush seating and a
well-stocked bar fill the intimate space. Here, the air hums with earnest
chatter as hopeful couples exchange their life stories over the likes
of It's Not What You Think It Is (it's tequila, vermouth and Campari).

A TABACARIA

Map 2; Rua de São Paulo 75/77, Cais do Sodré;
///buckets.rebirth.slurs; 930 697 413

Where tobacconists once advised their customers on cigars and
pipes, master mixologists now suggest cocktails. At the chunky
wooden counter, the mustachioed bartenders ask their laid-back
patrons about their mood and preferences before carefully crafting

bespoke cocktails. It's a slow but mesmerizing process – these personalized concoctions are worth the wait.

» **Don't leave without** popping across to super-popular Lupita Pizzeria to grab a pizza. A Tabacaria is happy for its customers to eat take-out while they wait for their cocktails.

O BOM O MAU E O VILÃO

Map 2; Rua do Alecrim 21, Cais do Sodré; ///acute.pebble.tonic;
www.obomomaueovilao.pt

Cais do Sodré is generally all about cheap student hangouts and sweaty nightclubs, so this sexy cocktail bar is a bit of an outlier in these parts. Under the watchful gaze of pop-culture icons like Amy Winehouse, Superman and Clint Eastwood (the bar's named after the 1966 Spaghetti Western *The Good, the Bad and the Ugly*), a cool crowd listens to live music and DJ sets, while nursing the likes of Monkey Trouble – a curious mixture of gin, cucumber, basil, bitters and egg white. There's nothing bad or ugly about that.

Try it!
MIX YOUR OWN DRINKS

Making cocktails needn't be rocket science. Learn the tricks of the trade from master mixologists on a refreshingly unpretentious workshop at Ás de Copos (*www.asdecopos.com*).

Rooftop Bars

A drink tastes better with a great view, right? Well, good news: this hilly city has numerous rooftop bars where the beautiful, higgledy-piggledy skyline forms the perfect backdrop to an alfresco tipple.

PARK

Map 2; Calçada do Combro 58, Bairro Alto;
///flies.gather.headache; 215 914 011

Bairro Alto's worst-kept secret, Park is a local icon. Atop a big, ugly, multistorey car park, a mixed crowd of gawping tourists and too-cool-for-school locals gather to quaff cocktails and hustle to house music. The real draw, however, is the views: Lisboetas spend many an evening here, lingering over Aperol Spritzes and watching the sun slip beneath the patchwork of terracotta roofs.

TOPO

Map 1; Centro Comercial Martim Moniz 6 Esq, Martim Moniz;
///strictly.cabbage.diverts; 215 881 322

Move over Park; Topo is the coolest rooftop bar in town these days. Why? Its cocktails are creative (no Aperol Spritzes here). Its food menu is far more expansive (think veggie gyoza, tuna tartare

and pork cheek on a sweet potato mash). And its vibey soundtrack
is set by the resident DJ, rather than Spotify. The unobstructed views
of the Castelo de São Jorge are the cocktail cherry on top.

» Don't leave without ordering the Clapton Cocaine. Nothing illegal
here, just good ol' vodka, raspberry liqueur, lemon, cinnamon,
strawberry and egg white.

FERROVIÁRIO

Map 6; Rua de Santa Apolónia 59, Alfama; ///shocks.running.banter;
www.grupochamp.pt

Ferroviário has had many lives. In the 1960s, it was a social club for
Lisbon's railworkers (hence the old company logo above the stage),
then a simple snack bar, and now it's one of the city's hottest
rooftops. And we mean hot – Ferroviário gives off serious holiday
vibes with its palm trees, wicker lampshades and lounge chairs.
It's the perfect place to soak up those 300 days of sunshine.

HOTEL MUNDIAL'S ROOFTOP BAR

Map 1; Praça Martim Moniz 2, Baixa; ///slacker.dweller.shadows;
www.hotel-mundial.pt

The Mundial has always been the place to be and be seen – this hotel
has hosted the likes of French writer Jean-Paul Sartre, bombshell
Brigitte Bardot and 007 himself, Roger Moore. And with its
monochrome colour scheme, plush sofas and back-lit bar, the
Mundial's rooftop bar gives off similarly hip vibes. Lisbon's coolest
gather here for after-work martinis (shaken, not stirred, of course).

Solo, Pair, Crowd

Found in shopping centres and concealed between buildings, these rooftop bars are hidden gems.

FLYING SOLO
Shop and sip

Take a break from shopping in El Corte Inglés and grab a cheeky drink at the rooftop Gourmet Experience. It's not got the best view in Lisbon, but it's a quiet alfresco spot to watch the world go by.

IN A PAIR
Petiscos for a pair

Enjoy a glass of wine – and the obligatory *petiscos* – with a pal at Terraço Editorial, on the top floor of the Pollux department store. Its west-facing terrace guarantees stunning sunset views over Baixa and Chiado.

FOR A CROWD
A historic happening

Order a round of drinks, grab a few of the bean bags and settle in for a chilled-out afternoon at Topo Chiado. It's a really great spot to see a couple of Lisbon's top sights, like the Elevador de Santa Justa and Convento do Carmo ruins.

TERRAÇO CHILL-OUT LIMÃO

Map 6; Avenida Duque de Loulé 83, Avenida; ///fenced.torn.game;
www.h10hotels.com

Lisbon is full of hotel bars, but this one feels extra special. Maybe it's the pretty, geometric blue-and-white tiled floors and killer sunset scenes. Or perhaps it's the fact that it's only open to non-guests when the sun is shining, which – fortunately – it almost always is.

JAVÁ

Map 2; Praça Dom Luís I 30, Cais do Sodré; ///recline.resemble.fetch;
935 945 545

Friends tell friends, who tell yet more friends, about this not-so-secret rooftop, hidden behind an unmarked door (tip: look for the little "30"). Here, they soak up the 360-degree views of the Tejo on one side and the pastel-pretty city on the other.

» **Don't leave without** ordering Javá's brunch board – a laden platter of Middle Eastern small eats. You'll need a big group to finish it.

V ROOFTOP BAR

Map 3; Rua Rodrigo da Fonseca 2, Príncipe Real; ///shoebox.official.lists;
www.thevintagelisbon.com

Get ready to channel your inner influencer because V is one of the most photogenic rooftops in Lisbon. Loungers, daybeds and cabanas sit against a "living wall" of succulents and mosses in a tiny space reminiscent of a secret garden. Speaking of gardens, we recommend ordering the English Garden (elderflower liqueur, apple juice and gin).

Iconic Quiosques

For Lisboetas, hardly a day goes by without stopping at a quiosque *(kiosk). In the morning, locals arrive early to quaff a* bica *at the counter. Come evening, they settle in for the long haul with beers and wine.*

QUIOSQUE DO CARMO

Map 1; Largo do Carmo, Chiado; ///gangway.deadline.fetch; 916 348 056

Overlooked by the earthquake-ravaged ruins of the Convento do Carmo, the Quiosque do Carmo has a picture-perfect setting. And, yes, that's probably why this classic green-and-white kiosk has become a bit of a tourist trap during the day. At night, however, it's a different story. Rock up after hours and join Chiado residents for lengthy catch-ups over port cocktails and jugs of sangria.

QUIOSQUE LISBOA

Map 3; Praça do Príncipe Real 19, Príncipe Real; ///bubble.jams.date; www.quiosquelisboa.pt

As the 9–5 draws to a close, Lisboetas swap endless emails and vexing video calls for the chilled surrounds of the Jardim do Príncipe Real, within which stands this all-time favourite. A sweat-beaded beer

Come here on a Saturday morning to catch the organic produce market in the surrounding garden.

or a revitalizing *mazagran* (sweetened espresso mixed with a hint of lemon zest) help to shake off the trials of the working day.

BANANA CAFÉ

Map 1; Doca da Marinha, Baixa; ///player.stressed.division

The three (yes, three) Banana Cafés on the revamped Doca da Marinha naval yard look very different to Lisbon's quintessential *quiosques*. The architecture – minimalist glass cubes with splashes of bright neon – might not be to everyone's taste, but having a drink while soaking up riverfront views of the Tejo is a definite crowd-pleaser.

» Don't leave without popping inside the nearby ferry terminal to admire the impressive *azulejos*, depicting Portuguese coats of arms.

QUIOSQUE CLARA CLARA

Map 4; Jardim Botto Machado, Alfama; ///clock.pebbles.maker; 218 850 172

When lunchtime rolls in, Alfama's young professionals inevitably make their way to Quiosque Clara Clara. At the shaded, green tables, they talk business (or, more likely, their after-work plans) over oozing mozzarella, brie or goats' cheese toasties, while enjoying the views. And what views they are. With the white-domed National Pantheon on one side (where Lisbon's great and good are buried) and the sparkling Tejo on the other, it's more than a struggle to return to the office.

QUIOSQUE DE SÃO PAULO

Map 2; Praça de São Paulo, Cais do Sodré; ///camper.mulls.toxic

What was once a down-and-out tipple stop for Cais do Sodré's rowdy sailors is now a polished red *petisco* spot. It's all the work of local hero, chef André Magalhães. And while it's hard to nab a table at his Taberna das Flores, you're almost always guaranteed a seat on the shady terrace here.

» Don't leave without trying the delicious fried squid sandwich, served with sriracha mayo. Wash it down sailor-style with a *ginjinha*.

QUIOSQUE RIBADOURO

Map 3; Avenida da Liberdade; ///circular.origin.resides; www.cervejariaribadouro.pt

On scorching hot days, glammed-up girlfriends only have one place in mind: Quiosque Ribadouro. At this classic green hut, they order a round of quenching drinks and plenty of seafood platters, before taking a seat at one of the parasol-cooled tables. There's no better way to while away the afternoon.

QUIOSQUE DO ADAMASTOR

Map 2; Rua de Santa Catarina, Bairro Alto; ///faster.nodded.exactly

Okay, most locals bring their own bottle of wine with them to watch the sunset at Miradouro de Santa Catarina. But when they've forgotten the obligatory BYOB (or want to impress a first date), Quiosque do Adamastor is an excellent second-best.

Liked by the locals

"Kiosks are a big part of daily life in Lisbon: everything from informal business meetings to jam sessions happens beside them. And they've become even more popular during the pandemic because they're in the fresh air."

ANNA GRUBER, INVESTMENT CONSULTANT AND QUIOSQUE REGULAR

An afternoon of kiosks in
Avenida

Back in the 19th century, Lisboetas would pop by a *quiosque* on the regular to pick up the newspaper or sip a *bica*. By the turn of the century, however, these Art Nouveau stalls had fallen out of fashion and were all but abandoned until the late 2000s, when Catarina Portas – the owner of nostalgic brand A Vida Portuguesa *(p106)* – reopened one as a trendy café. Fellow entrepreneurs soon followed suit and now the city is littered with reimagined *quiosques*, serving up everything from humble *imperials* to fine-dining dishes. Hop between Avenida's diverse kiosks on this tour.

**Unwind at
QUIOSQUE
BECA BECA**

Sip a frothy cappuccino, good ol' *imperial* or fancy cocktail in the tranquil surrounds of Parque Eduardo VII.

1. Quiosque Beca Beca
Parque Eduardo VII,
Avenida
///inner.decreased.whispers

2. Quiosque Ribadouro
Avenida da Liberdade 155,
Avenida; www.cervejaria
ribadouro.pt
///circular.origin.resides

3. Banana Café
Avenida da Liberdade 18,
Avenida
///urban.observer.early

**4. Quiosque do Miradouro
de São Pedro de Alcântara**
Rua de São Pedro de
Alcântara, Bairro Alto
///clots.sandwich.teams

Elevador da Glória ///shield.brothers.behind

Parque
Eduardo

AMOREIRAS

LARGO
DO RATO

RATO

RUA DE SÃO BENTO

SÃO
BENTO

Dig in at
QUIOSQUE RIBADOURO

This *quiosque* is all about seafood. Savour a plate of garlicky clams or *sapateira recheada* (crab mixed with pickles and mayonnaise, and served in the shell).

2

Swing by
BANANA CAFÉ

Join the lively crowd here, who come to cheer on their football team with a beer in hand. When games aren't projected onto a giant screen, there's live music.

3

Have a sundowner at
QUIOSQUE DO MIRADOURO DE SÃO PEDRO DE ALCÂNTARA

It's a bit of a climb up to this kiosk (only tourists take the *elevador*), but the views are worth it – promise. Order a *bica* and soak up the sunset.

4

*The **Elevador da Glória**, which trundles up to Bairro Alto, was built around the same time as the city's traditional kiosks.*

PRAÇA MARQUÊS DE POMBAL

ANJOS

AVENIDA FONTES PEREIRA DE MELO

AVENIDA DUQUE DE LOULÉ

RUA GOMES FREIRE

AVENIDA DA LIBERDADE

RUA A. A. HERCULANO

RUA DO SALITRE

Jardim Botânico

Campo Mártires da Pátria

AVENIDA ALMIRANTE REIS

PRAÇA DA ALEGRIA

PRAÇA DO PRINCIPE REAL

RUA DOM PEDRO V

PRINCIPE REAL

ELEVADOR DA GLÓRIA

RUA SÃO PEDRO DE ALCÂNTARA

PRAÇA DOS RESTAURADORES

PRAÇA MARTIM MONIZ

MOURARIA

CHIADO

| 0 metres | 300 |
| 0 yards | 300 |

SHOP

In laid-back Lisbon, the locals like to shop slow – and we mean slow. Lisboetas take their sweet time browsing stores, invariably pausing at a kiosk along the way.

Gourmet Treats

*For Lisboetas, the best part of the weekly grocery run
is chatting over the counter. Independent food stores
are the lifeblood of Lisbon's shopping circuit, bringing
out the city's small-business spirit.*

MANTEIGARIA SILVA

**Map 1; Rua Dom Antão de Almada 1C and D, Baixa;
///modules.dressing.plants; www.manteigariasilva.pt**

With 365 recipes to work through, Lisboetas need a steady supply
of *bacalhau*. And Baixa *avós* (grandmas) have relied on Manteigaria
Silva for their daily cod – and local news report – since 1890. As
they take their pick from the heaving fish counter, hanging hams
and piled-high shelves of port, Silva's regulars share the latest gossip
from around the neighbourhood (so listen up if you speak Portuguese).

COMIDA INDEPENDENTE

**Map 3; Rua Cais do Tojo 28, Santos and Madragoa;
///pounce.blubber.freed; www.comidaindependente.pt**

"Big products, small producers" is Comida Independente's motto.
To ensure her deli counter is stocked with Portugal's best gourmet
groceries, store owner Rita Santos regularly travels across the

Meet the producers yourself at Comida Independente's market, held in Praça de São Paulo each Saturday.

country, jumping from meetings with olive farmers to tastings at cheese-mongers. Order the sandwich of the week to sample her latest foodie findings.

COMPANHIA PORTUGUEZA DO CHÁ

Map 3; Rua do Poço dos Negros 105, Santos and Madragoa;
///clusters.purist.elated; www.companhiaportuguezadocha.com

The Portuguese were catching up over a cuppa long before the English became obsessed with tea. In fact, it was Portuguese princess Catherine of Braganza who made the drink fashionable in England back in 1662. Today, her face is stamped on Companhia Portugueza do Chá's vintage-style tea caddies, which are filled to the brim with trusty breakfast blends, rare Japanese leaves and festive infusions.

» Don't leave without picking up a bag of special Portuguese blends to take home. Try the Azorean white tea or the Lisbon Breakfast, which mixes black tea from the Azores and Sri Lanka.

CONSERVEIRA DE LISBOA

Map 1; Rua dos Bacalhoeiros 34, Baixa; ///ignites.sting.rafters;
www.conserveiradelisboa.pt

It looks like a sweet shop in here, with row upon row of pretty printed packages filling the old wooden shelves. But instead of sweet treats, these tins encase preserved fish. That's not to say these savoury morsels aren't equally enticing – yes, there's your classic tins of tuna, but there's also the likes of spicy squid, smoky octopus and tangy mackerel.

MERCEARIA POÇO DOS NEGROS

**Map 3; Rua do Poço dos Negros 97/99, Santos and Madragoa;
///every.worked.dealings; 211 385 681**

Plastic-free wholefood stores were difficult to find in Lisbon before Mercearia Poço dos Negros opened in 2016. The zero-waste, healthy approach was an instant hit with eco-conscious locals, who come here on the regular to fill their totes with unpackaged grains, artisan breads and funky-but-tasty cheeses.

A MARIAZINHA

**Map 6; Avenida Rio de Janeiro 25B, Alvalade; ///rushed.dished.hotels;
www.amariazinhacafes.lojasonlinectt.pt**

When Alvalade mums and dads have out-of-towners visiting, they make a beeline for A Mariazinha to pick up supplies. This old-fashioned store has everything you need to act the perfect host:

Shh!

While many commuters rush out of Martim Moniz metro station, locals-in-the-know venture deeper below the surface. Hidden between the corridors that connect the metro to the dated Centro Comercial Mouraria shopping centre is the Popat Store (*www.popatstore.pt*), a one-stop shop for all things spicy. Here, Lisbon's large Indian community and those who like their food *picante* (hot, hot, hot) replenish their spice racks with the best imported ingredients.

posh tins of biscuits, and specially blended tea and coffee that's ground right in front of you. The Lote Extra, made up of 60 per cent Arabica and 40 per cent Robusta beans, is sure to impress any guest.

GINJINHA SEM RIVAL
Map 1; Rua das Portas de Santo Antão 7, Baixa;
///navy.packages.rent; 213 468 231

Though thousands of places sell *ginjinha*, a sour-cherry liqueur and Lisbon's pride and joy, this shot-sized store is where long-time Baixaites come for an early morning pick-me-up (it opens at 8am). As you approach, the larger-than-life owner asks *"com elas ou sem elas?"* over the counter. Don't stress: he's just asking whether you want a cherry in your glass – be careful, it won't be pitted.

» Don't leave without buying a bottle of the lesser-known house drink, the *eduardino*. Legend has it that this sour cherry and aniseed liqueur was named after a local clown who was once a regular customer.

MERCADO DA FIGUEIRA
Map 1; Praça da Figueira 10, Baixa; ///cracks.trading.ships; 211 450 650

After the 1755 earthquake took out the hospital on Praça do Figueira, enterprising Lisboetas set up food stalls on this square. The Mercado da Figueira, as it was named, soon became *the* place to buy groceries in the 18th century. Today, the central market is long gone, but this little gourmet store bearing its name continues its legacy. Local families pick up their essentials here, while students come to raid the wine alley before a big night out.

Book Nooks

Digital nomads are nothing new here; Lisbon has been a regular haunt for roving writers for centuries. It's fitting, then, that bookshops dot every neighbourhood, fuelling the creativity of the city's residents.

BOOKSHOP BIVAR

Map 6; Rua de Ponta Delgada 34A, Arroios; ///marked.tasters.fend; 935 328 672

Literature-loving Canadian Eduarda was onto a winner when she bought this spot, now Lisbon's most beloved English-language bookshop and freelancer hangout. This expat enclave is a home away from home: house plants, mismatched furniture and piles of used books give off serious living room vibes. It instantly makes

Try it!
WRITE ALL ABOUT IT

Writing can be a solitary profession, so why not join up with some like-minded folk at Lisbon Writing Group *(www.lisbonwriting group.wordpress.com)*? Aspiring authors and professionals all attend the regular meet ups.

everyone feel comfortable and sets a welcoming tone for Bivar's reading circles, writing clubs and book swaps, where new and long-time Lisboetas make friends over wine, beer and books.

TINTA NOS NERVOS

Map 3; Rua da Esperança 39, Santos and Madragoa; ///successor.summer.sprouts; www.tintanosnervos.com

If you're after a tome on Portuguese art to grace your coffee table, look no further than this carefully curated store. Behind the tiled façade, you'll rub shoulders with Santos's creatives, eagerly looking for inspiration between the pages of design books and artsy magazines. So eager, in fact, that they often can't wait to get home before they start reading, instead diving into their new book right away at the pastel-green tables out back.

» Don't leave without seeking more inspiration from the artworks on display in the light and airy adjacent gallery.

BAOBÁ

Map 5; Rua Tomás da Anunciação 26, Campo de Ourique; ///blurred.composer.braced; www.orfeunegro.org

With its cute and colourful wall murals, comfy reading corners and loyal little patrons, you'd be forgiven for thinking that Baobá only stocks kids' books. But you'd be wrong. As well as picture books, hot-off-the-press comics and graphic novels have a home here. It's a favourite with artsy adults, who are regulars at Baobá's Saturday readings and illustration workshops.

PALAVRA DE VIAJANTE

Map 3; Rua de São Bento 34, Estrela; ///barn.jetting.curve;
www.palavra-de-viajante.pt

When Lisboetas are in need of a holiday, they hotfoot it to this
cavernous store to feel one step closer to departure. Here, they
thumb through the travelogues, maps and guides (like this one,
ahem) and start plotting their next adventure.

LIVRARIA SIMÃO

Map 1; Escadinhas de São Cristóvão 18, Mouraria; ///snack.gift.strongly;
961 031 304

Welcome to the smallest bookshop in the world. Livraria Simão is
so tiny that owner Simão has to step outside so you can browse all
the spines. Don't let the store's diminutive size fool you – there's a lot
of books to browse here, with over 4,000 Portuguese paperbacks,
Spanish romances, English comics and rare Chinese poetry
anthologies crowding the towering shelves. Schedules are a bit
erratic, so give Simão a call to set up a visit.

LIVRARIA BERTRAND

Map 2; Rua Garrett 73/75, Chiado; ///parts.fork.cashier; www.bertrand.pt

Now owned by the Porto Editora chain, Livraria Bertrand has played
a key role in Lisbon's literary heritage. Founded way back in 1732 (it's
the world's oldest bookshop, don't you know), the storied shop has long
been the reading spot of choice for famed writers, and walking into
the *azulejo*-crusted building today feels like being a part of that

Every Saturday, a small book fair is held around the corner from the shop, with prices starting at €1.

history. While away a few hours browsing the huge collection alongside Lisbon's next generation of writers – city students, who often come here looking for set texts.

STUFF OUT
Map 3; Rua da Quintinha 70C, Estrela; ///choirs.answers.global; www.stuffout.pt

Bothered by the number of books that are thrown away after just one read, uni buddies Pedro and Rui quit their tech jobs to start this second-hand bookshop. Everything is about rescuing books from rubbish heaps here, from the pre-loved paperbacks on the shelves to the colourful feature wall papered with pages from ripped and unsellable tomes.

LER DEVAGAR
Map 5; Rua Rodrigues de Faria 103, Alcântara; ///slower.puzzles.ship; www.lerdevagar.com

Some books are rip-roaring page turners, while others should be savoured word by word. Ler Devagar is all about the latter – its name means "read slowly", after all. Bookworms take their sweet time skimming their fingers over the thousands of spines here, pouring over pages in the two café-bars and ogling at the jumping-puppet-style sculptures that hang from the ceiling.

» Don't leave without flicking (slowly, of course) through the jazzy records upstairs at Jazz Messengers.

Vintage and Thrift Stores

Lisbon has a long history of thrift shopping. Some of the city's feiras (street markets) have been popping up in the same squares since the 12th century, and the local love of a good bargain shows no sign of slowing.

A OUTRA FACE DA LUA

Map 1; Rua da Assunção 22, Baixa; ///info.samples.hogs;
www.aoutrafacedalua.com

Always lusted after a vintage kimono? Join Lisbon's 20-somethings at A Outra Face da Lua, which specializes in 1960s to 90s fashion. Think patterned headscarves, bright ski jackets, tie-dye sweats and, of course, delicate, silk kimonos.

CASA PÉLYS

Map 5; Rua Tomás da Anunciação 62, Campo de Ourique;
///rank.pink.welcome; 213 887 408

True antique shoppers love the thrill of the search, and locating the entrance to this second-hand store is a taster for the quest to come. (Hint: look for the faint Foto Pélys sign, a throwback to when this was a photographer's studio.) The hunt continues inside, where Campo de Ourique's newest flatmates rifle through buckets of used books, vintage lamps and biscuit boxes. Found something you like? The next challenge is to find the store's owner — he's usually in the café next door.

FEIRA DA LADRA

Map 4; Campo de Santa Clara, Alfama; ///hotdog.improves.honest
Every Tuesday and Saturday morning, vendors spread out blankets on the Campo de Santa Clara to hawk the likes of old-school toys, mismatched china and retro sunnies. Things can get pretty touristy and disorderly, but don't be put off as there are great deals to be had. Just ask the couple carrying their new painting home or the crate digger tightly clutching that rare record.

>> Don't leave without seeking out a busker when the chaos all gets too much. Brazilian samba or accordion-led Portuguese folk music will soon get you in the mood for another round of bargain-hunting.

RETRO CITY LISBOA

Map 4; Rua Maria Andrade 43, Arroios; ///shelters.found.shave; 218 099 932
When Arroios hipsters want to update their wardrobe, they head to Retro City to pick up someone else's once-treasured threads. This is the kind of place where your colleague found that cool bag they always carry and your best friend picked up those Levis that fit like a glove. It's packed to the rafters with pieces, so go when you have the time to really root through the rails.

POP CLOSET

**Map 1; Calçada do Sacramento 48, Chiado; ///scouts.football.shaves;
www.pop-closet.com**

Though Lisbon is a jeans-and-a-tee kind of city, Pop Closet flies
the flag for high-end, couture fashion. Owner António Branco,
a fashion industry veteran and once the editor of *GQ Brazil*,
personally curates the collection, picking up items like last season's
Fendi jacket, suede Chloé dresses and Chanel's iconic 2.55 bags.

TROPICAL BAIRRO

Map 1; Rua de São Cristóvão 3, Mouraria; ///dome.refuse.scraper

Vinyl and vintage: they just go together. Tropical Bairro is a record
and thrift store in one, so you can pick up an LP and a tee at the
same time. Owned by DJ and man-about-town Paolo Dionisi, it
attracts a solid crowd of Mouraria residents who appreciate Latin
beats and relaxed threads. We're talking bright bomber jackets,
oversized Hawaiian shirts and a whole lot of plaid.

FEIRA DO INTENDENTE

**Map 4; Largo do Intendente Pina Manique, Arroios;
///insect.opposite.stable**

Viúva Lamego, a 19th-century ceramics factory with one of the
best-decorated façades in Lisbon (and that's saying something),
provides a grand backdrop to this market, held on the second
Sunday of each month. Die-hard collectors arrive early, scanning the
stalls for treasures and scooping up timeworn porcelain, first-edition

Feeling the strain of hauling totes around? Swing by The Chilled Cat, the market's pop-up massage parlour.

books and rare comics. Later, teenagers roll in to check out the funky clothes stalls like Hardcore Fofo, which stitches swear words onto dainty crochet designs.

ÁS DE ESPADAS

Map 2; Calçada do Carmo 42, Chiado; ///retained.trees.shrimps; 916 789 199

The darling of the Portuguese fashion press, Ás de Espadas is where trendy Chiado locals go to purge and replenish their wardrobes with sartorial treasures from the 1930s through early 2000s. Look out for treasures like demure 1920s bathing suits, 1960s-era Mary Jane heels and loud and proud 1980s earrings.

» **Don't leave without** checking out the sunglasses collection. If you thought you didn't need another pair, prepare for a major rethink once you clap eyes on these 1960s and 70s beauties.

HUMANA

Map 6; Avenida de Roma 3, Avenidas Novas; ///surviving.proud.century; www.humana-portugal.org

Conveniently located near campus, this outpost of the European charity store chain is stocked and shopped by Universidade de Lisboa students. It has a constant turnover, but you can always count on finding Adidas trainers, a perfectly distressed pair of denim shorts and an oh-so-perfect outfit to wear the next time you hit the dance floor. Bonus point: Humana's profits fund social projects around the world.

Record Stores

You're never too far from a strumming busker, spinning DJ or soulful fado singer here. Little surprise, then, that Lisbon's record stores are some of the most popular places in the city.

DISCOTECA AMÁLIA

Map 1; Rua Áurea 272, Baixa; ///fiction.fairness.cheaper

What, you ask, is fado? It's hard to pin down. The best way to get to grips with this melancholic music is to listen to it, and Discoteca Amália is a good place to start. Named after Amália Rodrigues, aka the queen of fado, this little shop stocks the classics as well as new records from the likes of Mariza, Carminho and Cuca Roseta.

CHASING RABBITS

Map 3; Rua do Sol ao Rato 61A, Campo de Ourique; ///craters.wiser.grudge; www.chasingrabbitsrecordstore.com

When vinyl-collecting students fancy a laidback Sunday afternoon, they swing by this record store and café. Here, they browse the collection of new and second-hand alternative, indie and rock sleeves from the likes of Bowie, Fontaines D.C. and Velvet Underground, on the hunt for their new favourite album. Hours are easily lost here but if hunger strikes there's no need to move on: Chasing Rabbits doubles as a restaurant, serving up fortifying veggie burgers, loaded nachos and codfish cream cakes.

» Don't leave without exploring the hot chocolate menu. Flavours include coconut, whisky and the very Lisbon *pastel de nata*.

CARBONO
Map 3; Rua do Telhal 6B, Avenida; ///hatter.laptops.loafer; www.carbono.com.pt

Of course a second-hand record store dedicated to heavy metal started life in a dark and dank basement. As the crates began to overflow, Carbono moved onwards and upwards (literally) to this spacious Avenida store. But the collection and clientele remain the same, with kohl-eyed rockers still leafing through LPs by the likes of Black Sabbath and Megadeth.

CARPET & SNARES
Map 2; Rua da Misericórdia 14 , Chiado; ///demand.flirts.surfed; www.carpetandsnares.com

The small shopping gallery Espaço Chiado is a treasure trove for vinyl nerds, with three record stores to choose from: Peekaboo, Sound Club and Carpet & Snares. All three are worth a visit but if you're into techno and dance music, make a beeline for Carpet & Snares. This record label has been pushing Lisbon's techno soundscape to a cult-like following since 2014, releasing tracks, hosting in-store parties and running workshops on how to DJ or produce music.

FLUR

Map 6; Rua Ângela Pinto, Arroios; ///modest.backers.secrets; www.flur.pt

Few visitors – and locals – know that Brazilian, Cape Verdean and Angolan rhythms and beats have been just as important as fado in shaping Lisbon's soundscape. Flur flies the flag for that lineage by partnering with Príncipe Discos, a label dedicated to releasing dance music produced by the city's minority communities.

LOUIE LOUIE

Map 1; Escadinhas do Santo Espírito da Pedreira 3, Chiado; ///infuses.guides.grew; www.louielouie.biz

Records fill every nook of Louie Louie, even the ceiling. And this eclectic store stocks just about every genre imaginable, from classical to disco, Brazilian samba to American jazz. If you're feeling overwhelmed, the friendly owners will happily put you on the right track.

AMOR RECORDS

Map 4; Rua Frei Francisco Foreiro 2A, Arroios; ///fewest.arena.pumps; 964 535 586

Amor feels more like a social club than a record store. The furniture is mismatched, there's an on-site bar pouring craft beer and everyone seems to know each other. Arrive to flick through the records and you'll soon get drawn into a lively discussion on the best reggae, Afrobeat or Brazilian record ever made.

» Don't leave without sifting through the discounted section to grab an LP for as little as €1.

Liked by the locals

"The days when you could strike vinyl gold simply by rocking up at Lisbon's flea markets are long gone. If you're a real collector and looking for fair prices, you will find them in Lisbon, but you have to know where to look. I love to go to Amor Records."

LUIZ BENEVIDES, STUDENT AND RECORD COLLECTOR

Home Touches

Lisboetas are a crafty bunch, whipping up azulejos and blankets as if it were nothing. If this doesn't sound like you, no worries: the city is full of stores where you can pick up characterful pieces, made with TLC.

ICON

Map 2; Rua Nova da Trindade 6B, Chiado; ///example.melons.nuggets; www.iconshop.pt

In a city of crafters and artists, a store like Icon makes sense. Here, Portuguese artisans show off their work in the pop-up studio space. Right before your eyes, metal is twisted into delicate jewellery, a mound of clay slowly transforms into a ceramic bowl and black-and-white sketches become colourful prints.

BUREL FACTORY

Map 2; Rua Serpa Pinto 15B, Chiado; ///altering.mental.gossip; www.burelfactory.com

High up in the mountains of the Serra da Estrela, deep in the heart of central Portugal, shepherds wear *burel*. Made from Bordaleira sheep wool, this traditional fabric is incredibly comfortable, warm and water-repellent – characteristics that Isabel Dias da Costa and

João Tomás valued while on a hiking trip to the mountains. On their return to Lisbon, the business partners invited young designers to take a contemporary twist on this age-old fabric, and Burel Factory was born. The store still sells up-and-coming designers' interpretations of *burel* – think fuzzy rugs, comfy footstools and quirky vases.

» **Don't leave without** checking out Burel Factory's collaboration with Sanjo, the historic shoe brand, for some seriously warm footwear.

CORTIÇO & NETOS
Map 4; Rua Maria Andrade 37D, Arroios; ///spout.punks.willing;
www.corticoenetos.com

Azulejos are synonymous with Lisbon, and the perfect souvenir. For the biggest selection of designs, head to Cortiço & Netos. Former owner Joaquim Cortiço spent years amassing *azulejos* from all over Portugal, sneaking in orders just before many factories closed down in the 1990s. Alongside these rare, discontinued designs are fresh, modern motifs chosen from the remaining factories by Joaquim's *netos* (grandkids), who now run the family business.

Try it!
MAKE YOUR OWN

Can't find your perfect *azulejo* at Cortiço & Netos? Create your own design at Casa do Azulejo (*www.acasadoazulejo.pt*). Workshops range from two-hour tile-painting classes to year-long *azulejo*-making courses.

CLAUS PORTO

**Map 2; Rua da Misericórdia 135, Chiado; ///replied.trunk.bets;
www.clausporto.com**

No Chiado bathroom is complete without a cabinet full of Claus Porto
soaps and perfumes. Drop into this gorgeous store, set in an old
pharmacy, to inhale the scents that this heritage brand has been
bottling since 1887. You'll leave with a bagful of deliciously fragrant
presents for your friends (and, let's be honest, yourself).

CERÂMICAS NA LINHA

**Map 2; Rua Capelo 16, Chiado; ///odds.subjects.confirms;
www.ceramicasnalinha.pt**

When roommates move into their first apartments, they come to
Cerâmicas Na Linha to stock up on crockery. Here, colourful plates,
funky bowls and curvaceous mugs are made locally and sold by the
kilo, so new homemakers can add a characterful stamp to their
home without breaking the bank.

A VIDA PORTUGUESA

**Map 4; Largo do Intendente Pina Manique 23, Arroios;
///magnetic.credit.toxic; www.avidaportuguesa.com**

A Vida Portuguesa has made it easier than ever to buy Portuguese
crafts. This well-curated store stocks everything you can think of,
as long as it's made in Portugal and has withstood the test of time:
intricately embroidered napkins, carefully crafted carpentry and
jugs shaped like roosters (the symbol of Portugal). You'll come to

buy a printed notebook for a birthday gift and leave with a classy collection of ceramics for your next dinner party (and a wicker bag, because you need something to take them home in, right?).

» Don't leave without pausing in front of the *azulejo*-bedecked façade of ceramic factory Fábrica Viúva Lamego next door.

DEPOZITO

Map 4; Rua Nova do Desterro 21, Arroios; ///span.approach.hesitate; www.avidaportuguesa.com

A collab between A Vida Portuguesa and Portugal Manual, Depozito is a celebration of Portuguese style old and new. While A Vida Portuguesa is all about old-school handicrafts, Portugal Manual flies the flag for contemporary designers, like illustrator Tiago Galo and ceramicist José the Potter. A dedicated following of Arroios creatives go gaga for the eclectic stock, like modern, origami-style light fixtures and traditional *azulejos* that have been turned into coasters.

Apart from Depozito, the only other place to get your hands on Portugal Manual's iconic, contemporary designs is at the pop-up store in CCB (Centro Cultural de Belém). Hidden away inside the box office, this small space stocks around 40 brands from Portugal Manual's huge network of designers. Swing by to nab a unique vase or rug that will make any visitor to your home ask "where did you find that?"

Indie Boutiques

A Lisboeta's style may be pretty casual, but locals are serious about where they shop. They've ditched chains in favour of the true gems: indie stores, where each piece of apparel is locally designed and made.

+351

Map 2; Rua da Boavista 81C, Cais do Sodré; ///prosper.airports.hops; www.plus351.pt

Cais do Sodré's sun-, sea- and surf-loving residents perfect their comfortable-chic look at +351. Everything from the cosy, organic cotton hoodies to the gold-plated earrings are unisex, ready-to-wear and made right here in Portugal. At €45 for a plain white T-shirt, it isn't cheap but these basics are made to last the ravages of time and ever-revolving trends.

LUVARIA ULISSES

Map 1; Rua do Carmo 87A, Chiado; ///tilt.boomed.badly; 213 420 295

Back in the 1920s, fashionable Chiado residents came to Luvaria Ulisses to get their gloves – essential accessories in those days. Times may have changed but tradition is hard to shake, and a loyal band of regulars still come here to purchase the finest Portuguese

There's a right way to try on a glove: soften it with talcum powder, then rest your elbow on the counter.

leather gloves. The fun, brightly coloured designs are year-round crowd-pleasers, while colder months call for cashmere-lined winter warmers.

EMBAIXADA

Map 3; Praça do Príncipe Real 26, Príncipe Real; ///scarf.stubble.quick; www.embaixadalx.pt

Welcome to Lisbon's fashion embassy. In 2013, this Neo-Moorish palace transformed from a hotel into a shopping gallery (despite its name, it never housed diplomats). Today, the sumptuous rooms are occupied by designers who represent the Portuguese fashion scene. Expect a rotating roster of stores, with too-pretty-to-get-wet swimwear on offer one visit and organic cosmetics the next.

» Don't leave without refuelling with Middle Eastern-style dishes at Casa Cabana, one of the many restaurants that has a residency here.

A FÁBRICA DOS CHAPÉUS

Map 2; Rua da Rosa 118, Bairro Alto; ///arrives.soils.exist; www.afabricadoschapeus.com

If you're looking for something to keep the sun out of your eyes – and there's a lot of sun in Lisbon – you'll find it at A Fábrica dos Chapéus. Wander in and you'll see towers of fancy fedoras, quirky berets, wide-brimmed hats and many more stylish creations lining the shelves. If you still can't find a style that suits you, talk to the friendly owner, who will happily design a custom creation. Hats off to that!

Liked by the locals

"The fashion scene here in Lisbon is incredibly exciting. I'm constantly amazed by how Portugal's strong sense of tradition is effortlessly combined with contemporary manufacturing techniques to produce really unexpected styles."

ALEXANDRA JOLIE SU, FASHION DESIGNER

LES FILLES

Map 3; Travessa do Rosário 33A, Príncipe Real; ///litters.keepers.soap; www.lesfill.es

Lisboetas may be known for their pared-back style, but not everyone is a fan of the utilitarian look. Sequin-loving Joana Bernardo and Maria João Fialho certainly aren't, so expect plenty of daytime glitz and glamour at their boutique, Les Filles.

THE FEETING ROOM

Map 1; Calçada do Sacramento 26, Chiado; ///overhaul.unroll.smallest; www.thefeetingroom.com

Portuguese leather is world famous and The Feeting Room is all about celebrating this local material in a modern way. Here, black loafers are spiced up with fur overlays, court shoes balance on architectural heels and sneakers are given a metallic coating.

» Don't leave without grabbing a flat white, when you need a pick-me-up, at SO Coffee Roasters, the in-store café.

LA PAZ

Map 2; Rua das Flores 16, Cais do Sodré; ///prime.panting.rescue; www.lapaz.pt

Newsflash: the lumberjack look is so last season. It's all about the fisher look now. La Paz dresses Lisbon's salty sailors and seafaring wannabes in the latest nautical threads (anchor-logoed tees, fleece-lined jackets and chunky turtlenecks designed to keep off the Atlantic Ocean chill are firm favourites).

The **Assembleia da República** *(Portugal's parliament)* is housed in the grand *Palácio de São Bento*, on the outskirts of the Triangle.

RUA DA CRUZ DOS POIAIS

LA
DE

CALÇADA DA ESTRELA

Find your style at
MINI MALL

Peruse this eclectic shop for alternative fashion, quirky Portuguese handicrafts and Moroccan rugs that will bring a splash of colour to your home.

5

RUA DOS POIAIS DE SÃO BENTO

Pick up a book at
PALAVRA DE VIAJANTE

Leaf through guidebooks and memoirs for inspiration at this cosy travel bookshop.

4

RUA DE SÃO BENTO

Pop by
MERCEARIA POÇO
DOS NEGROS

Pick up an afternoon snack at Mercearia Poço dos Negros, which stocks fresh bread, artisan jams and local cheeses.

RUA DO POÇO DOS NE

3 **2**

Browse at
COMPANHIA
PORTUGUEZA
DO CHÁ

Looking for the perfect gift for your tea-loving friend? Scour this old-fashioned store's wooden shelves, brimming with thousands of different blends.

RUA DA SILVA

Its real name is Rua da Silva, but after being flooded with plant pots by residents, this stretch has been christened **Lisbon's Green Street.**

LARGO DO CONDE BARÃO

0 metres	100
0 yards	100

An afternoon of shopping in
the Triangle

Drawn by low rents, creative folks started setting up shop on Rua Poiais de São Bento, Poço dos Negros and Rua de São Bento in the mid-2010s. Since then "the Triangle" has become a byword for the city's hippest corner. Think buzzy brunch spots, speciality coffee outlets, indie bookshops and, of course, cute plant stores.

Fuel up at
THE MILL
Grab some brunch and a flat white at this Aussie-style café (yes, Vegemite's on the menu). Love the plate you're eating off? You're in luck – the ceramics are all on sale.

1. The Mill
Rua do Poço dos Negros 1, Santos and Madragoa; www.themill.pt
///retrial.braked.workouts

2. Mercearia Poço dos Negros
Rua do Poço dos Negros 97/99, Santos and Madragoa; 211 385 681
///every.worked.dealings

3. Companhia Portugueza do Chá
Rua do Poço dos Negros 105, Santos and Madragoa; www.companhiaportugueza docha.com
///clusters.purist.elated

4. Palavra de Viajante
Rua de São Bento 34, Estrela; www.palavra-de-viajante.pt
///barn.jetting.curve

5. Mini Mall
Rua Poiais de São Bento 120B, Estrela; 938 480 441
///waitress.deform.image

Lisbon's Green Street
///bake.fountain.freed

Assembleia da República
///internal.life.tabloid

RUA DA BOAVISTA

TRAVESSA DO ALCAIDE

ARTS & CULTURE

From 18th-century azulejos *pasted onto earthquake-ravaged ruins to politically charged street art grabbing the city's attention, Lisbon is all about creativity.*

City History

Lisbon wouldn't be the place it is today without its historic trials. Between earthquakes, dictatorships and economic woes, the city has been tested again and again, and emerged more resilient every time.

CONVENTO DO CARMO

Map 1; Largo do Carmo, Chiado; ///prove.staring.multiple;
www.museuarqueologicodocarmo.pt

To get to grips with the full force of Lisbon's famous 1755 earthquake, visit the Convento do Carmo. This once grand, 14th-century convent was ravaged to skeletal ruins by the disaster. If the remaining walls could talk, they'd have plenty to say – and talk they do each summer, when the convent becomes the stage for a sound-and-light show that re-creates the earthquake's impact.

PADRÃO DOS DESCOBRIMENTOS

Map 5; Avenida Brasília, Belém; ///bland.physical.touchy;
www.padraodosdescobrimentos.pt

Portugal has a way of putting the "Age of Discoveries" on a pedestal, and nothing reflects the glorifying of imperialism more than this 1960s trophy monument to 15th- and 16th-century navigators. Following the toppling of similar statues across the world, Padrão dos Descobrimentos was tagged with the words "Blindly sailing for money, humanity is drowning in a scarlet sea" in 2021. The vandalism stirred up debate in a country still coming to grips with its colonial past and bolstered plans to build a museum that would address the uncomfortable realities of colonialism.

MUSEU NACIONAL DO AZULEJO

Map 6; Rua da Madre de Deus 4, Marvila; ///coder.reserve.plotting; www.museudoazulejo.gov.pt

Lisboetas will tell you that this city is always evolving, and nowhere exemplifies its ever-changing face quite like the Azulejo Museum. Home to thousands of salvaged tiles that once adorned buildings, this is a catalogue of a Lisbon lost to natural disasters, despots and time. **» Don't leave without** taking in the Grande Panorama de Lisboa, which shows what Lisbon looked like before the 1755 earthquake.

MUSEU DO FADO

Map 1; Largo do Chafariz de Dentro 1, Alfama; ///encoder.values.rating; www.museudofado.pt

Some say fado started as sailors' shanties, others claim it was inspired by the songs of enslaved African people. However it began, it's clear that this melancholy music, which is infused with *saudade* (a sort of longing for something or someone far away), reflects this city's seafaring past. Check out Museu do Fado's exhibitions, concerts or guitar workshops to learn more.

AFRICAN LISBON TOUR

Map 1; Praça do Comércio, Baixa; ///feelers.found.recorder;
www.africanlisbontour.com

Brush up on Lisbon's oft-ignored Black history by booking onto the
African Lisbon Tour. Designed by Togo-born Naky Gaglo, the walk
brings a more rounded world-view than the many city tours on offer,
explaining Lisbon's role in the slave trade, and inviting guests to enjoy
a Cape Verdean meal and dance to some Afrobeats.

MUSEU DO ALJUBE

Map 1; Rua Augusto Rosa 42, Alfama; ///shots.registry.owes;
www.museudoaljube.pt

Salazar's former prison is a symbol of both oppression and liberty
for Lisboetas. Today, its cells hold exhibitions rather than political
prisoners, describing the torturous techniques that jailers used and
the origins of the Carnation Revolution. The what revolution? Its

Shh!

Take a surprising dive into 2,500
years of history beneath the
Baixa branch of Millennium
BCP. A 1990s renovation
unearthed Iron Age, Roman and
Visigoth remains beneath the
bank, and now free, hour-long
tours take in the underground
site. (Tours in English are held
roughly on the hour.) Although
few visitors have heard of the site,
you'll have to show up early to
bag one of the few spots *(www.
fundacaomillenniumbcp.pt).*

story is as Lisbon as it gets: on 25 April 1974 Salazar and his 41-year dictatorship were overthrown by a military coup without a drop of blood being shed. The revolution's name came about because locals placed carnations into the soldiers' guns as a symbol of their support.

PARQUE DAS NAÇÕES

Map 6; Parque das Nações; ///caravan.change.shared

Lisbon brought the world together for the 132-day Expo '98, with countries erecting pavilions across the purpose-built Parque das Nações site. Today, this area still connects people around the globe during the annual Web Summit – but it's also a place where people live, and residents are proud of what their neighbourhood has become.

MOSTEIRO DOS JERÓNIMOS

Map 5; Praça do Império, Belém; ///powerful.lance.sensual;
www.mosteirojeronimos.pt

A Portuguese monastery might sound like a strange place to get to grips with the country's imperial history, but hear us out. This vast and flamboyant building was funded by a tax on the trade of cinnamon, ginger and other spices from Portugal's African and Asian colonies. As a nod to its beginnings, the architects of Mosteiro dos Jerónimos incorporated maritime, Asian and African symbols into their designs. Look out for carved ropes, lions and even a mermaid.

» Don't leave without popping into nearby Pastéis de Belém, where the cinnamon-sprinkled *pastéis de nata* are still made to the original recipe crafted by Jerónimos monks.

Public Art

Lisbon has long been home to colour-splashed streets. From centuries-old azulejos to ever-evolving canvases where budding graffiti artists make a statement, there's always something different to see.

OFERENDA

Map 6; Rua Alberto José Pessoa, Marvila; ///remotes.evening.trash

Marvila is full of abandoned warehouses and peeling façades – it's basically one big, blank canvas. And that's exactly why the neighbourhood was chosen to host the annual Festival Muro, when local and visiting street artists splash the walls. Lisboetas can't resist swinging by to see what's new and admire old favourites, like Portuguese artist Kruella D'Enfer's 2017 addition *Oferenda*, a surreal image of a vase bursting with Ibero-American plants and wildlife.

LX FACTORY

Map 5; Rua Rodrigues de Faria 103, Alcântara;
///window.brightly.topping; www.lxfactory.com

Set in creatively minded Alcântara, this textile factory-turned-artsy hub is where Lisbon's coolest come to mosey around at the weekend. The former weaving rooms on the upper floors now house edgy studios but many artists prefer to try out new styles on the walls at street level. Start just inside the gates, in front of a giant 3D bee made entirely from rubbish by superstar artist Bordalo II. What comes next as you walk around the complex changes on every visit but you can bet on seeing some bold and beautiful graffiti.

» **Don't leave without** popping into Samantha Wilson Art, one of Lx Factory's many studios. Check out the Scottish artist's work or sign up for a class to create your own masterpiece.

DESASSOSSEGO

Map 4; Rua Damasceno Monteiro, Graça; ///among.skips.without

Every Lisboeta read the works of Fernando Pessoa at school, including street artist Akacorleone, who has immortalized the enigmatic writer's face in bold, Picasso-style colours on a wall in Graça. Is Akacorleone's bespectacled creation silently judging the folks below or thinking about his next poem? Just like its subject, this portrait is wonderfully hard to pin down.

CALÇADA

Map 1; Rua São Tomé, Alfama; ///critic.embedded.restless

Stop staring at the *azulejos* and start looking down at Lisbon's *calçadas*. Lisbon's traditional cobblestone pavements are patterned with waves, stars and other geometric designs. Well, usually. In 2015, Portuguese street artist Vhils transformed one such pavement, with the help of the city's municipal team of pavers, into a mosaicked tribute to the late fado diva (and Alfama hero) Amália Rodrigues.

UNIVERSAL PERSONHOOD

Map 4; Rua Senhora da Glória, Graça; ///moats.scrap.answers

Two titans of the international street art scene came together to create this politically charged piece. One half is painted in the bold colours of American artist Shepard Fairey (creator of Barack Obama's "Hope" campaign poster), while the other is carved into the wall itself – a technique made famous by Portuguese artist Vhils. The thought-provoking result is a Muslim woman simultaneously with and without her hijab, revealing her universality. It's a skewering statement against the Islamophobia sometimes encountered in this city.

LARGO RAFAEL BORDALO PINHEIRO 30

Map 2; Largo Rafael Bordalo Pinheiro 30, Chiado; ///upholds.adjust.driver

Politically motivated public art isn't new. Take the *azulejo*-clad façade of Largo Rafael Bordalo Pinheiro 30, in which 19th-century artist Luis Ferreira hid Masonic symbols. The all-seeing "eye of providence" looks down on six classical figures, representing the four elements, science and agriculture. What does it all mean? No one knows, but it's a conversation starter, at least.

IBERIAN LYNX

Map 6; Rossio dos Olivais, Parque das Nações;
///stormy.corals.adopting; www.bordaloii.com

You've heard the phrase "one man's trash is another man's treasure", and now's your chance to judge if it's true. Using everything from scrap metal to old fishing nets, Portuguese artist Bordalo II creates giant 3D portraits of native animals. In 2019, he crafted his masterwork, a towering, rainbow-hued sculpture of the endangered Iberian lynx. It's creative and a little bit quirky, which is exactly why Lisboetas love it.

» Don't leave without journeying underground to check out the water-inspired murals in nearby Oriente metro station. Many stations have similar works so keep your eyes peeled as you move around the city.

MURAL DE AZULEJOS
Map 4; Largo Dr Bernardino António Gomes, Alfama;
///kicked.reminds.tutored

For decades, *azulejos* were considered seriously old-school by the Lisbon art world. That was until André Saraiva created this thoroughly modern mural from over 50,000 hand-painted tiles in 2016. Instead of rural or religious scenes made up of traditional blue, yellow, and white tiles, Saraiva's rainbow-bright mural chronicles his urban and irreverent life in Lisbon, Paris and New York. Spot the box of matches, bottles of wine and signature scrawled post-it note.

Try it!
GRAB A CAN

Leave your mark in Lisbon by booking a spray-painting workshop with Lisbon Street Art Tours *(www.lisbonstreetarttours.com)*. You'll spend the afternoon learning spray-painting techniques from a pro.

Favourite Art Museums

Where do Lisbon's many crafters and creators go to get inspired? The city's brimming art museums. Here, they join a discussion, take a workshop or check out the exhibition everyone's talking about.

MUDE

Map 1; Rua Augusta 24, Baixa; ///across.landed.twilight; www.mude.pt

Stylish, fashion-forward Lisboetas love the Museum of Design and Fashion, a design powerhouse that's hosted sell-out exhibitions dedicated to the likes of Balenciaga, Jean-Paul Gaultier and Alexander McQueen. Although the building is currently closed for renovations, MUDE continues to run regular exhibitions elsewhere through MUDE Fora de Portas (MUDE Outside Doors).

MUSEU COLEÇÃO BERARDO

Map 5; Praça do Império, Belém; ///form.pockets.help; www.museuberardo.pt

Lisbon's flag bearer for 20th-century art, the Museu Coleção Berardo is home to paintings by all the big names (think Picasso, Miró and

Hop on the tram to Belém on Saturday, when entrance to the Berardo's permanent collection is free.

Warhol). Add first-class exhibitions from lesser-known artists, like Julian Opie and Miguel Palma, and it's no wonder Lisboetas trek out to Belém on the regular.

MUSEU NACIONAL DE ARTE ANTIGA

Map 3; Rua das Janelas Verdes, Santos and Madragoa;
///princes.royal.late; www.museudearteantiga.pt

While this powerhouse of a museum is stuffed with Portuguese paintings, Chinese ceramics and African art, it's the exhibitions that keep locals coming back, like 12 Escolhas, when 12 celebrities picked 12 items from the collection. You can still find their choices online – discover why designer Christian Louboutin chose a folding screen, and why actress Monica Bellucci was so taken with a statue of St Michael.

IMMERSIVUS GALLERY

Map 3; Praça das Amoreiras 10, Príncipe Real; ///fool.included.moved;
www.lisboa.immersivus.com

Subterranean water reservoirs are usually dark, dank and uninspiring places. Not so in Lisbon. This reimagined reservoir is one of the city's most atmospheric and inspiring gallery spaces, hosting sound and light shows. Past installations have seen works by Impressionist Claude Monet and Symbolist Gustav Klimt projected simultaneously onto the dripping stone pillars and reflected in the water below.

» Don't leave without climbing up to the viewing platform on Reservatório da Mãe d'Água's roof to see the huge aqueduct below.

FUNDAÇÃO CALOUSTE GULBENKIAN

Map 5; Avenida de Berna, 45A, Avenidas Novas;
///patting.promoted.reaction; www.gulbenkian.pt

It's Saturday, you've yet to make plans and you're in the mood for a culture kick. Make a beeline for the Fundação Calouste Gulbenkian. This museum is actually two institutions, housed in separate buildings: the Museu Calouste Gulbenkian, which has a collection stretching back to antiquity, and the cutting-edge Centro de Arte Moderna. So, if you want to brush up on the development of Islamic art, it's got you covered. Prefer video art? It's got you there, too.

MUSEU NACIONAL DE ARTE CONTEMPORÂNEA DO CHIADO

Map 2; Rua Capelo 13, Chiado; ///request.chills.padlock;
www.museuartecontemporanea.gov.pt

Nestled amid Chiado's cool indie boutiques and creative businesses is this local favourite, which often attracts a stylish crowd of regulars on their lunchbreak. Join them as they check out exhibitions on

Try it!
LEARN TO DRAW

Brush up your drawing skills with the Lisbon Drawing Club (*clubedesenholisboa@gmail.com*). Classes and workshops are organized by local creatives and usually held at an artist's house or atelier.

subjects like Tomás da Anunciação's romantic landscape paintings or the experimental video work of Alexandre Estrela, and then mull it all over in the courtyard café.

MUSEU DE ARTE, ARQUITETURA E TECNOLOGIA

Map 5; Avenida Brasília, Belém; ///singers.spoons.laws; www.maat.pt
How does the pop art movement connect to the invention of the refrigerator? The Museum of Art, Architecture and Technology (or MAAT to its friends) aims to find out. Rotating exhibitions explore all kinds of topics, like whether robots have feelings and if video games could save us from extinction (spoiler alert: MAAT thinks they already have).

>> Don't leave without taking a moment on MAAT's riverside steps to reflect on what you've just seen inside.

CORDOARIA NACIONAL

Map 5; Avenida da Índia, Belém; ///dirt.outraged.steps;
www.patrimoniocultural.gov.pt
There are three things that Lisboetas love about Cordoaria Nacional. First, the headline-grabbing exhibitions from the likes of British graffiti giant Banksy and Brazilian photojournalist Sebastião Salgado. Second, the building's history (and Lisboetas sure love history) as a rope-making factory for the navy. And third, the stunning location on the shimmering Tejo, with the golden 25 de Abril Bridge and hilltop Cristo Rei statue looming large in the background.

Indie Art Galleries

With its magical light, creative history and low living costs, it's no wonder that so many artists call Lisbon home. And where there are artists, there are indie galleries repping their work.

GALERIA MALAPATA

Map 1; Rua Nova do Almada 9, Baixa; ///gravest.directly.galleries; www.malapata.pt

Forget cheap posters from Baixa's tacky and overpriced souvenir shops and instead upgrade your home with a funky limited-edition print from Galeria Malapata. A hotspot for art graduates and upcoming illustrators (you may even spot some proud patrons gazing up at their own art on display), this tiny gallery sells affordable (prices are rarely in three figures) artworks to pop on your wall.

UNDERDOGS GALLERY

Map 6; Rua Fernando Palha 56, Marvila; ///claims.thin.breathed; www.under-dogs.net

It won't come as a surprise that there's a gallery dedicated to graffiti in Lisbon's hipster heartland. Works by street artist Vhils (who founded Underdogs back in 2010) may get mural-obsessed Marvilans through the doors here, but it's the cutting-edge exhibitions that make them stay. Everything on display has a questioning take on society, like Wasted Rita's feminist light installations or ±MaisMenos±'s anti-capitalist pieces.

» Don't leave without grabbing a post-art drink at one of Marvila's many craft breweries. Try Bo Brewpub, Dois Corvos or Lince.

ZARATAN

Map 3; Rua de São Bento 432, Estrela; ///hooked.imposes.wrong; www.zaratan.pt

An art gallery in an old charcoal factory? How appropriate. Since an enterprising group of artists took over the building in 2014, Zaratan has become the vanguard of the Lisbon creative scene, responding to shifting trends in the art world. The non-profit is all about exhibiting fresh artists and out-there installations – you know, like a collection of objects found along Rua de São Bento or a live performance where an artist flattens cans with a hammer.

GALERIA SÃO MAMEDE

Map 3; Rua da Escola Politécnica 167, Príncipe Real; ///pyramid.miles.yell; www.saomamede.com

Way back in 1968, when Galeria São Mamede first opened, Salazar was squashing all independent thought and anti-dictatorship art. So, how did this cutting-edge gallery evade closure? Sheer luck. And Lisboetas count themselves lucky in turn that it's still exhibiting such thought-provoking photography and sculptures today.

Solo, Pair, Crowd

Whether you've got the day to yourself or you're exploring with the gang, there's a gallery for you.

FLYING SOLO
Pick up a print

Looking for something unique to hang on your walls? Swing by the Centro Português de Serigrafia, a cultural centre dedicated to the art of screen-printing, to find the perfect print for your apartment.

IN A PAIR
Join the discussion

You and your date will have a lot to talk about after taking in one of Perve Galeria's thought-provoking exhibitions. Luckily this youth and cultural association is surrounded by cafés where you can digest what you've just seen over a cup of coffee.

FOR THE CROWD
Cultured crowd

There's always something cool going on at Carpintarias de São Lázaro. So, check the calendar, gather the gang and get ready to see some experimental art. Oh, and be sure to grab a drink on the rooftop terrace.

HANGAR

Map 4; Rua Damasceno Monteiro 12, Graça; ///flooding.lazy.encounter; www.hangar.com.pt

Lisbon's student crowd loves a debate, and that's exactly why they're such big fans of Hangar. As well as conversation-sparking exhibitions, this cavernous indie hosts seminars that are guaranteed to provoke conversation, on topics like the role of radio in Cold War Angola and whether craft beer can reflect the immigrant experience.

» Don't leave without signing up for a workshop. Subjects range from how to take the perfect photograph to the art of radio.

ARTROOM

Map 2; Pátio do Tijolo 1, Príncipe Real; ///replied.bolts.swan; 968 516 630

Hidden away in an attic, this gallery is only frequented by those in the know. See that door plastered with stickers on Pátio do Tijolo? Yes, that's the entrance. Upstairs, you'll find some of the freshest names on Lisbon's contemporary art scene. Check Artroom's social pages to find out exactly who's on display right now.

GALERIA 111

Map 6; Campo Grande 113A, Alvalade; ///rapport.bend.zest; www.111.pt

Thanks to the promotion of talents like Maria Helena Vieira da Silva and Paula Rego by art dealer Manuel de Brito, Galeria 111 became synonymous with young Portuguese artists in the 1970s and 80s. Today, the city's wannabe art critics still flock here to see the next big names in Portuguese art.

Get Crafty

Lisbon is a city of crafters. In their downtime, locals love perfecting their hobby or learning something new – whether that's how to knit a sweater, screen-print a tote bag or paint azulejos.

CORRENTE

Map 4; Rua Passos Manuel 99A, Arroios; ///channel.bright.sticky

This co-working space hums with the chatter of girlfriends catching up and creative nomads brainstorming projects. Run by Leonor Loureiro, who's known for directing super-cool, narrative fashion films, Corrente is all about creating unique and fashion-forward pieces, like a pair of funky, psychedelic trousers or a tote bag appliquéd with a punch-needled kiwi fruit. Check out its socials to find out which workshops are on when.

FÁBRICA MODERNA

Map 6; Rua Pereira Henriques 5, Marvila; ///bristle.wiping.onions; www.fabricamoderna.com

Just like in Lisbon itself, technology and tradition intersect at this hands-on workspace. Lasers and 3D printers sit alongside old-school woodwork stations and kilns, and seasoned solderers meld jewellery next to newbies designing their best friend's wedding invites. It's pretty popular with Marvila's creative crowd, so sign up early if you have your sights set on a specific class.

FICA

Map 4; Rua de Arroios 154B, Arroios; ///cutlets.appendix.taped;
www.fica-oc.pt

Arroios's transformation from a deprived neighbourhood into an artsy hub is thanks to small ceative businesses like this one. Fica is all about passing on traditional techniques to others. It's the work of owner and craft-obsessive Rita Rodrigues, who leads lino print, woodwork and clay-work classes.

» Don't leave without grabbing a bite to eat at nearby Kerala *(p45)* with your new buddies after class.

SEDIMENTO

Map 3; Travessa Santo Ildefonso 31, Estrela; ///snores.warm.parade;
www.sedimento.pt

Tired of spending hours in front of laptops, web designer Maud Téphany and architect Úrsula Duarte swapped their keyboards for kilns and started making ceramics. Úrsula now makes crockery for Lisbon's top restaurants, while Maud's ceramic balloons and ice creams can be spotted around town. Feeling inspired to give up your desk-bound day job, too? Sign up for a ceramics course at their studio, Sedimento. You'll learn how to make a vase, dessert bowls or even a set of ceramic birds.

RETROSARIA ROSA POMAR

Map 4; Rua Maria Andrade 50A, Arroios; ///tweeted.spines.trunk;
www.retrosaria.rosapomar.com

Newsflash: knitting is cool, especially when you pick up a pattern for a skater-style beanie and balls of hand-spun neon yarn from Rosa Pomar. Don't know your knit from your purl? Don't worry, this haberdashery runs masterclasses and personal consultations.

CERÂMICA SÃO VICENTE

Map 1; Rua de São Vicente 31, Alfama; ///deeper.clashes.swear;
www.ceramica-svicentelisboa.com

At Cerâmica São Vicente's paint-splattered table, mother-and-son team Cristina Pina and Miguel Moura teach Alfama couples and out-of-towners how to design, paint and fire their very own ceramic tiles – the perfect souvenir from the city of *azulejos*.

A AVÓ VEIO TRABALHAR

Map 6; Largo Mendonça e Costa 10, Arroios; ///gourmet.wake.shelf;
www.fermenta.org

Who better to learn crafts from than a grandma? At A Avó Veio Trabalhar, *avós* teach the next generation of makers and shakers how to embroider, screen-print and craft paper flowers, while recounting their life stories. (The young founders, Susana and Ângelo, are on hand to translate for English crafters.)

» **Don't leave without** asking the *avós* about the time they modelled at Lisbon Fashion Week. Yes, these grandmas are cooler than you.

Liked by the locals

"Lisbon is a city where past and future live side by side. This is obvious in the world of crafts, where you often see entrepreneurs and inventors alike slowing down with knitting, embroidery and other crafts."

ANA ISABEL RAMOS, ILLUSTRATOR, DESIGNER AND
KNITWEAR DESIGNER AT AIR DESIGN STUDIO

An artsy afternoon in
Arroios

For decades, Arroios had a bad reputation for drug dealing and gang culture, a plight that worsened with the fall of Salazar's regime in 1974. Creative folks didn't start moving into the 'hood until 2001, when Portugal decriminalized drugs and the local government cleaned up the streets (and compensated those who made the move). Since then, Arroios has seen rapid gentrification but, between the boutique hotels and trendy bars, an alternative spirit still burns, with cool record shops, artists' studios and politically engaged street art on every corner.

1. Mercado de Arroios
Rua Ângela Pinto, Arroios
///rots.emerald.quit

2. Fica
Rua de Arroios 154B,
Arroios; www.fica-oc.pt
///cutlets.appendix.taped

3. Tabatô Records
Rua de Arroios 11B, Arroios;
961 626 144
///vivid.advising.stars

4. Cortiço & Netos
Rua Maria Andrade 37D,
Arroios; www.corticoe
netos.com
///spout.punks.willing

 Corrente
///channel.bright.sticky

 Fábrica Viúva Lamego
///vent.youth.spreads

SALDANHA

PRAÇA
DUQUE DE
SALDANHA

AVENIDA FONTES PEREIRA DE MELO

AVENIDA DUQUE DE LOULÉ

AVENIDA DA LIBERDADE

Tuck into lunch at
MERCADO DE ARROIOS

Tickle your tastebuds with
Syrian dishes from Mezze,
freshly baked pizzas at
Margarita or barbecued chicken
from the on-site *churrascaria*.

If *Fica* is booked up,
try **Corrente**, which
organizes workshops
on the likes of crochet
and punch needle.

Get crafty at
FICA

Embrace your inner artist at this
creative studio, which hosts
regular ceramics, woodwork
and screen-printing classes.

Pick up some vinyl at
TABATÔ RECORDS

French DJ Selecta Orka celebrates
the diversity of Lisbon's music scene
at his record store. Dive into the
crates to score a great Portuguese,
Brazilian or African LP.

Browse the tiles at
CORTIÇO & NETOS

Pick up the quintessential Lisbon
souvenir, an *azulejo*, at Cortiço &
Netos. The collection includes
some rare designs, so you might
go home with a unique find.

Fábrica Viúva Lamego
*stopped producing
ceramics long ago,
but its stunning
19th-century tiled
façade remains.*

RUA A. P. CARRILHO

RUA MORAIS SOARES

ARROIOS

AVENIDA ALMIRANTE REIS

RUA PASCOAL DE MELO

PRAÇA PAIVA COUCEIRO

RUA DE DONA ESTEFÂNIA

RUA PASSOS MANUEL

RUA DE ARROIOS

RUA DA PENHA DE FRANÇA

AVENIDA GENERAL ROÇADAS

PENHA DE FRANÇA

RUA F. MONIZ

AVENIDA ALMIRANTE REIS

RUA ANDRADE

ANJOS

RUA A. VIDAL

LARGO DO INTENDENTE PINA MANIQUE

0 metres   300
0 yards   300

NIGHTLIFE

Nights out in Lisbon start late and keep going well past dawn. Locals hop between intimate gigs, raucous raves and bars that spill out into the streets.

Late-night Bars

A true Lisboeta would never walk into a club as soon as the doors opened. Locals start their nights out in a classically laid-back fashion, crawling between bars until they're voguishly late to the party.

LOUCOS E SONHADORES

Map 2; Rua da Rosa 261, Bairro Alto; ///slumped.hint.glow; 213 471 339

Locals usually only pop into Bairro Alto's bars to grab an *imperial* (small beer) before retreating back onto the street outside to drink it. Loucos e Sonhadores is different. Students settle into its wonderfully kitsch interior, complete with dismantled mannequins, for the long-haul. Just one *imperial* soon turns into three as they pick at bowls of free popcorn and catch up on last night's gossip.

BACCHANAL

Map 2; Rua do Corpo Santo 28, Cais do Sodré;
///discouraged.fended.changed; 939 016 160

Cais residents looking to avoid the crowded bars and clubs on Rua Nova do Carvalho (aka Pink Street) make a beeline for Bacchanal. As the name suggests (Bacchus was the Roman god of wine), this place is all about *vinho*. The glass-fronted cabinets, repurposed

Swing by nearby Petiscaria do Elevador for a pre-drink and snack before moving on to Bacchanal.

from this building's old drug store days, overflow with Portuguese bottles. But if that's not your poison, the bartenders can whip up a mean cocktail, too.

ONDA

Map 4; Rua Damasceno Monteiro 45, Graça; ///strength.watched.bigger; 938 468 380

This city has a way of getting under your skin, and that's exactly what happened to Dubliner Peter O'Connor, a master mixologist, who opened a late-night bar just two days into his holiday in Lisbon. He soon gained a following of chic Graça girlfriends, who while away an hour or two sipping bespoke cocktails on the leafy terrace.

BOTEQUIM

Map 1; Largo da Graça 79, Graça; ///expose.tequila.jobs; 218 888 511

Way back when poet and political activist Natália Correia opened this bar in 1968, it hosted *tertúlias* (literary gatherings). Intellectuals came here to discuss the latest novel and freely conspire against Salazar's regime (it was called Botequim da Liberdade – the Freedom Tavern – at the time). When the dictatorship fell, the bar seemed redundant and closed down, but in 2010 Botequim was reborn. Today, it's a favourite once more of artists and writers, who come here for friendly debates over carafes of wine and rounds of *petiscos*.

» Don't leave without ordering a *café com cheirinho* – coffee with an *aguardente* (brandy) kick – if you're planning on debating into the night.

GALA GALA

**Map 1; Rua dos Douradores 120, Baixa; ///turkeys.author.risk;
937 911 946**

Sometimes we can't help but pine after decades gone by. Take the 1980s, when Lisbon had just emerged from its dictatorship and arcade games were all the rage. Gala Gala is an ode to that fun and liberated era. Here, nostalgic hipsters fritter away the hours before hitting the club playing Pac Man or Donkey Kong tournaments to a synth-pop soundtrack. Whoever loses buys the next round of beers.

BOUTIQUE TABERNA

Map 1; Escadinhas de São Cristóvão 8, Mouraria; ///exacted.final.fleet

You can't avoid climbing up and down hills on a night out in Mouraria. Luckily, there's a watering hole on every street, where you can pause and catch your breath. Plonked at the top of Escadinhas de São Cristóvão, a particularly calf-punishing set of stairs, Boutique Taberna refreshes puffed-out revellers with chilled Caipirinhas. There are very few tables, but who needs them when you can perch on the steps and listen to the buskers playing beside the *Fado Vadio* mural, a colourful portrait of local fado stars. It's hard to leave, but the next bar calls.

TROBADORES

Map 1; Rua de São Julião 27, Baixa; ///install.runs.fairly; 218 850 329

One of the few late-night watering holes in nightlife-starved Baixa, Trobadores has become the TGIF venue of choice for the area's 9-to-5ers. It's easy to forget the stresses of the working week when you're drinking craft beer from a hunting horn. Huh? If you hadn't guessed from the rustic, candlelit setting, live folk music (yes, that is a minstrel playing the bagpipes) and the servers' medieval outfits, this tavern is committed to its Middle Ages theme.

» **Don't leave without** trying a cup of *hidromel*. It's rare to find this traditional Portuguese mead in this city.

O BAR MAIS TRISTE DA CIDADE

Map 3; Calçada Ribeiro Santos 25, Santos and Madragoa;
///playoffs.path.infants; www.obarmaistristedacidade.com

When Lisboetas want to indulge their *saudade* (an untranslatable word somewhere between nostalgia and melancholy), they join the collective pity party at "The Saddest Bar in the City". Here, they nod knowingly along to the singers belting out 1980s power ballads and nurse comforting whiskey cocktails, served with a sympathetic smile. They might arrive feeling a little sad, but after spending some time among the glitzy mirror balls, fabulous retro furnishings and shimmering tinsel curtains, it's hard not to leave happy.

Try it!
LEARN THE ART OF FADO

Indulge your *saudade* even further by learning how to sing fado, write lyrics or play the Portuguese guitar at a workshop at the Museu do Fado *(www.museudofado.pt)*. Classes are all in English.

Live Music

Down to party? Lisbon's got you covered with pumping DJ sets, jubilant Angolan semba *and mosh-pit-worthy metal. (There's fado too, of course, if you're feeling nostalgic for a past partner or pal.)*

TASCA DO CHICO
Map 2; Rua do Diário de Notícias 39, Bairro Alto;
///starring.milder.replaces; 961 339 696

Despite what some say, Lisboetas don't listen to fado on the regular. When *saudade* does hit, however, booking a table at Tasca do Chico is a must. In the poster-plastered interior, a wine-quaffing crowd sit at gingham-covered tables, waiting for the guitarists and *fadista* (singer) to take to the floor and treat them to an emotional performance.

ZÉ DOS BOIS
Map 2; Rua da Barroca 59, Bairro Alto; ///prompting.bronzed.fried;
www.zedosbois.org

Shiny with perspiration, grown-up scenesters jump to the sounds of indie rock, groove to new wave and rap along to alternative hip-hop at ZDB (no one calls this non-profit art centre Zé dos Bois). Set in a former palace, with peeling plaster, almost non-existent lighting and the muggy scent of sweat, it's got all the hallmarks of the venues you worshipped as a teenager, minus the angst.

» Don't leave without checking out what else is on that night. Elsewhere in the building, ZDB hosts art exhibitions, theatre and dance performances, and rooftop cinema screenings.

DAMAS

Map 1; Rua da Voz do Operário 60, Graça; ///budget.renamed.wash; 964 964 416

While the uninitiated tuck into *petiscos* in the restaurant up front, a motley crowd slink past them to Damas's back room. Follow suit and you'll find a secret stage, hosting free gigs. It's hard to predict who'll be playing here – one night, it could be your mate's earnest experimental band, the next a jubilant Afrobeat act – but you can always count on banging tunes and a good time.

B.LEZA

Map 2; Cais Gás 1, Cais do Sodré; ///wiring.erase.styled; www.bleza.pt

Due to Portugal's far-reaching colonial empire, Lisbon is home to large Cape Verdean, Angolan, Mozambican and São Toméan communities. And when these first- or tenth-generation immigrants want to reconnect with their roots, they come to B.Leza to groove to Cape Verdean *funaná* or Angolan *kizomba* and *semba*. There's a lovely multi-generational vibe, with sprightly silver-haired couples showing off their moves to tripping millennials with two left feet.

Solo, Pair, Crowd

No matter who you're rolling with, Lisbon has something for every music lover.

FLYING SOLO

Make some new friends

Head over to Valsa, a small bar and music venue that promotes Luso-Brazilian artists, and feminist and LGBTQ+ causes. You're sure to get chatting to some of its spirited regulars between sets.

IN A PAIR

A traditional evening

Book a table for two at Maria da Mouraria. Set in the former home of late *fadista* Maria da Severa, this *casa do fado* (fado house) has all the ingredients of a perfectly Portuguese evening – *saudade*-filled sets and plates of *petiscos*.

FOR A CROWD

Dinner and dancing

The peppy sounds of *semba* and tantalizing scent of *moamba* (a traditional Angolan chicken stew) greet you as you walk through the door of Casa Mocambo. Gather the gang and get ready to hit the dance floor.

RCA CLUB

**Map 6; Rua João Saraiva 18, Alvalade; ///mixture.extra.crunchy;
www.rcaclub.com**

If you're looking for a mellow fado session, you've come to the wrong
place. RCA Club is all about head-banging hardcore rock. Local
metal-heads, sporting band tees, gather here to rock out to their
favourite local bands and rock tribute acts.

CASA INDEPENDENTE

**Map 4; Largo do Intendente 45, Arroios; ///trim.decrease.wharfs;
www.casaindependente.com**

Casa Independente's gigs are so epic that the city's creative crew
are happy to queue to get into this crumbling mansion (a rarity in
this laid-back city). Once inside, it's straight to the Tiger Room, which
hosts jazz, electronic and indie names.

» Don't leave without retreating to the leafy outdoor patio to catch
your breath and cool down between sets.

HOT CLUBE DE PORTUGAL

**Map 3; Praça da Alegria 48, Avenida; ///snails.complains.flows;
www.hcp.pt**

One of the oldest jazz clubs in Europe, Hot Clube de Portugal has
witnessed some legendary performances since it opened its doors
in 1948. It draws a solid crowd every night, with old-timers arriving
early to grab their favourite table and young jazz fans lining the
walls at the back (be prepared, it can get cramped).

LGBTQ+ Scene

Laid-back Lisbon welcomes everyone with open arms, however they identify. The city is full of inclusive venues, from high-octane clubs to mega-mellow bars, all promising a truly fabulous night out.

FRIENDS

Map 2; Travessa da Água da Flor 17, Bairro Alto; ///fancy.crunchy.flames; 924 309 235

Friends offers the best of both worlds. In the evening, it has a relaxed vibe with pals chatting over cocktails and tapas, and flicking through the books scattered across the tables. Come midnight, when the DJ hits the decks, things are turned up a notch, with students rocking up to make some moves (and see if the sign promising a "hot barman inside" was right).

TRUMPS

Map 3; Rua da Imprensa Nacional 104B, Príncipe Real; ///dubbing.leaflet.dissolve; www.trumps.pt

The parties at Lisbon's go-to gay club are so legendary that someone even wrote a book about them (look up Rui Oliveira Marques's *Histórias da Noite Gay em Lisboa*). The fun-loving crowd – mostly fashion-forward fellas, but also drag queens, go-go dancers and allies – get down to house music in one room, and chart and cheese in the other.

>> **Don't leave without** checking out Trumps Queer Art Lab. Apart from hands-in-the-air boogying, Trumps promotes queer art through exhibitions, lectures and workshops.

FINALMENTE CLUB

Map 3; Rua da Palmeira 38, Príncipe Real; ///broccoli.stewing.coached; www.finalmenteclub.com

Helmed by local drag legend Deborah Krystall, Finalmente has been showing people of all stripes a good time since 1976. A loyal flock return again and again for the camp lip-synced numbers from Deborah and her merry band of performers, plus all the sequined smocks you could wish for. Come in the early hours: the queens only take to the stage around 4am and it's a final frontier post for young guns who keep the party going till well past dawn.

SIDE BAR

Map 2; Rua da Barroca 33, Bairro Alto; ///rankings.bangle.weedy

If you're after a messy night, keep on walking past this pint-sized bar. Casual *imperial* and a friendly atmosphere more your thing? Make Side Bar your home for the evening. In classic Bairro Alto style, here folks take their drinks to the street outside, where strangers fast become friends as the night goes on. You'll soon be dancing together on the impromptu dance floor.

PRIMAS

Map 2; Rua da Atalaia 154, Bairro Alto; ///threaten.opposite.dominate;
213 425 925

Lesbian bars are thin on the ground in Lisbon, so Primas has
become the staple hangout for the community (though allies are
always welcome). Step inside and you're likely to be roped in to
a table football game or a round of shots.

CENTRO LGBT

Map 1; Rua dos Fanqueiros 40, Baixa; ///organic.wishing.lectures;
www.ilga-portugal.pt

This safe and inclusive community space is the work of the
Intervenção Lésbica, Gay, Bissexual, Trans e Intersexo (ILGA),
Portugal's oldest association for LGBTQ+ rights. It'll come as no
surprise then that Centro LGBT runs a diverse nightly programme
of cultural and political activities. Impassioned folk sign up for its

Shh!

Many people don't know about
Lisbon's booming burlesque
scene, with tassels twirling in
clandestine venues across the
city. It's all thanks to local star
Lady Myosotis, who produces
and hosts Lisbon Underground

Burlesque. Check social or email
(lisbon.underground.burlesque@
gmail.com) to find out when and
where the burlesque troupe is
next performing. Then gather
the crew and get ready for a
fabulous night.

book clubs or debates on LGBTQ+ issues, while creative kids join the improv theatre workshops or raucous karaoke nights. On a more serious note, Centro LGBT also offers essential services for the city's LGBTQ+ community, like a documentation centre, counselling sessions and support groups.

SHELTER BAR

Map 3; Rua da Palmeira 43A, Príncipe Real; ///servants.molars.poems; www.shelterbarlisboa.com

If the bearded bartenders don't give it away, maybe hairy mascot Bobo Bear will. Yes, this is Lisbon's beloved bear bar, although all are welcomed here with open arms. From Monday to Friday, it's pretty relaxed, with 9-to-5ers chatting to the cute bears at the next table over happy-hour craft beers. Weekends , on the other hand, call for a proper knees-up – think DJs, glitter balls and drag queens.

» Don't leave without browsing the Bobo Bear tees. This shirtless character was created by Italian illustrator Roberto Nisi.

POSH CLUB

Map 3; Rua de São Bento 157, Estrela; ///strapped.stews.elephant; www.poshclub.pt

On Friday and Saturday nights, Posh Club becomes the hottest place in town. Literally: this is Lisbon's go-to gay club for sweaty dancing. All-night partiers press closer and closer together as they groove to a soundtrack of house, funk and techno, spun by Posh's resident DJs.

Cool Clubs

Lisboetas aren't ones to show off, but even they'll admit that their city's club scene is pretty epic. Whether you're looking for a samba dance-off or a hardcore techno rave, you'll find it in Lisbon.

MUSICBOX

Map 2; Rua Nova do Carvalho 24, Cais do Sodré;
///lookout.protects.curtains; www.musicboxlisboa.com

Musicbox is the epitome of the Cais do Sodré's nightlife scene: groovy music, an underground vibe (it's in the arches beneath Rua do Alecrim) and a dance-til-dawn MO. A cool crowd rolls up around 2am, ready to sweat, smile and dance to smooth Afro-electronic tunes or jazzy *cumbia* (Colombian folk) until long past 5am.

LUX FRÁGIL

Map 4; Avenida Infante Dom Henrique Armazém A, Alfama;
///prongs.upstairs.sizes; www.luxfragil.com

The constant queue outside this old riverside warehouse speaks for itself – Lux likes to keep things exclusive. What else would you expect from a club once owned by Hollywood royalty John Malkovich? Your best shot at getting in is to come early (in Lisbon that means any time before 2am) and smile sweetly at the famously surly bouncers. Entry granted, it's straight to the dance floor to groove to the likes of heavy techno or 1980s bangers. If you're all about discovering up-and-coming DJs, swing by on a Thursday.

>> Don't leave without going up to the terrace to check out the sweeping views over the Tejo river. The last partiers standing head here at the end of the night to watch the sunrise.

NOIR CLUBBING
Map 6; Rua António Patrício 13B, Alvalade; ///drain.speaking.tooth

Scenesters were devastated when alternative Club Noir was pushed out of Baixa by rising rents, so imagine their joy when they found out it was making a comeback in Alvalade. The name may be slightly different, but the vibe is exactly the same. On Fridays, a long-haired and black-clad crew tramp in for heavy metal; Saturdays bring a pastiche of goths, indie kids and New Romantics.

INCÓGNITO
Map 3; Rua Poiais de São Bento 37, Santos and Madragoa; ///heap.scrap.arrives

To get into Incógnito, you'll need to get past D'Artagnan. Since he got the job in 1998, the mustachioed doorman has become an influential figure on Lisbon's nightlife scene, opening the doors to the likes of Iggy Pop and Nick Cave. Most days, though, he just lets in the club's TGIF-happy regulars, who come here to shake off their troubles to indie, synth-pop and new wave tracks.

LOUNGE

Map 2; Rua da Moeda 1, Cais do Sodré; ///bunny.then.sprinkle; www.loungelisboa.com.pt

It's impossible to predict what kind of music will be pumping out of schedule-free Lounge. It could be good ol'-fashioned rock 'n' roll, Latin beats or obscure disco tracks. Lisbon's student population are big fans of the musical roulette concept (and the fact that whatever the jam, entry is always free).

DESTERRO

Map 4; Calçada do Desterro 7, Arroios; ///outpost.sample.wicket

This basement club feels like a house party. Everyone seems to know each other, embracing like old friends and jumping to the relentless beat of electro. Don't be put off by its members-only status: the small entrance fee will get you a whole year of club nights, as well as artsy concerts, screenings and workshops.

» Don't leave without signing up for a spot at Wednesday's Desterronics, when musicians improvise a new electronic track.

TITANIC SUR MER

Map 2; Cais da Ribeira Nova, Cais do Sodré; ///drips.took.declines; 938 833 532

In 2015, an old fish market was transformed into this place, a modern cabaret club, hosting live music and dance acts – think smooth jazz musos, sexy samba dancers and earnest indie rockers. The most popular act? It's got to be Beyoncé Fest, a tribute to Queen B herself.

Liked by the locals

"When I'm DJing and look at the dance floor, I see people of all ages, from 18 to 70; people of all tribes, from goths to rastas, rockers to ravers; and people of all origins, all dancing together and having fun."

TIAGO ANDRÉ AKA A BOY NAMED SUE,
DJ ON LISBON'S CLUB SCENE

Cultural Spaces

Think of a community centre, and dry, neighbourhood gatherings might come to mind. Not so in Lisbon. These spaces are seriously cool hangouts, where locals catch artsy films or belly-laugh to stand-up comedy.

LISBOA COMEDY CLUB

Map 6; Avenida Duque de Loulé 3A, Avenidas Novas;
///outfit.credible.corded; www.lisboacomedyclub.pt

It's fair to say that Lisboetas don't have a reputation for being funny, but Lisboa Comedy Club is on a mission to change that. Every night of the week, the line-up of big names and up-and-comers tell their best jokes to an after-work-happy crowd. Don't speak Portuguese? Roll up on a Sunday for English night.

BUS PARAGEM CULTURAL

Map 4; Rua Maria 73, Arroios; ///precautions.sleep.premiums;
218 131 190

Arroios is well-known as an alternative nightlife hotspot, and BUS was one of the first on the scene when it opened in 2013. Its underground space hosts everything from swanky vegan dinner parties to hot-and-sweaty gigs, raucous quiz nights to

Continue your night out at nearby Crew Hassan, an edgy bar that hosts alternative DJ sets.

mellow yoga classes. It's all a bit makeshift, there's graffiti on the walls and it tends to get rather smoky, but hey, this is Arroios.

CAMONES CINE BAR

Map 4; Rua Josefa Maria 4B, Graça; ///today.enhanced.comfort; 933 297 441

Visiting this cosy spot is like popping over to your best mate's flat for a quiet night in. Owner Cláudia Loureiro has done a fine job of channelling living-room vibes with comfy sofas and beanbags, mismatched cushions and throws, and plenty of quirky flea-market touches. Come to watch the latest film everyone's talking about or listen to whoever's got the mic that night.

» Don't leave without signing up for a spot on open-mic night, if that's your kind of thing. This place welcomes singers, spoken word poets and comedians with open arms every Tuesday.

RUA DAS GAIVOTAS 6

Map 3; Rua das Gaivotas 6, Santos and Madragoa; ///recipient.skater.copycat; www.ruadasgaivotas6.pt

Lisboetas are heading back to school. Occupying an old primary school in Santos , this cultural centre puts on thought-provoking readings, avant-garde exhibitions and subversive performances by resident theatre company, Teatro Praga. Most of the events are in English, but confirm at the box office.

Solo, Pair, Crowd

Whether you're flying solo or hanging out with the gang, you're guaranteed to make new friends at these centres.

FLYING SOLO
See a flick
Share your take on the latest critically acclaimed movie at Curious Monkey's weekly film club. This small, community-run cultural space, just a short walk from the Sé cathedral, runs bilingual sessions.

IN A PAIR
Go indie
Catch an artsy movie with a friend at Cinema Ideal, a small independent cinema in Chiado. Afterwards, discuss what you've just watched over *petiscos* and glasses of *vinho tinto* in the on-site café.

FOR A CROWD
Dance it out
The more the merrier at Espaço Baião, a Brazilian dance school. Gather your mates and learn some *forró* or samba moves to bust out next time you hit the club together.

ARROZ ESTÚDIOS

Map 6; Avenida Infante Dom Henrique, Marvila;
///darling.padding.sentences; www.arrozestudios.pt

Arroz Estúdios is practically a neighbourhood itself, with over 8,000 members, 14 studios, two galleries, a co-working space, an outdoor pizzeria and a garden (phew, we got there in the end). Guitar-toting students join its jam nights, long-time couples take salsa classes and the curious check out new tech at the AR and VR exhibitions.

» Don't leave without looking to see what's on next at Black Cat Cinema, the open-air movie nights held in the garden.

FÁBRICA BRAÇO DE PRATA

Map 6; Rua Fábrica de Material de Guerra 1, Marvila;
///textiles.across.loaders; www.bracodeprata.com

At this gigantic, old munitions factory, culture and education are used as weapons for social change. Look out for skewering poetry slams, talks on subjects like the impact of Orientalism and family-friendly plays that address the perils of climate change.

VILLAGE UNDERGROUND

Map 5; Avenida da Índia 52, Alcântara; ///trouser.decisive.wells;
www.vulisboa.com

Settings don't get much cooler than Village Underground's. Crouched beneath Ponte 25 de Abril, these graffiti-splashed shipping containers and buses host indie film screenings, performance art installations and offbeat plays.

A night out in
Cais do Sodré

Once the city's docklands, Cais do Sodré was where sailors came to let off steam, hopping between brothels and grotty watering holes. Things are a lot more swanky than sleazy nowadays thanks to Time Out, who transformed a 19th-century fish market into a gourmet food hall in 2014, attracting foodies from far and wide. Today, former brothels house cocktail bars and old fish auctions have been made into nightclubs.

1. Javá
Praça Dom Luís I 30, Cais do Sodré; 935 945 545
///recline.resemble.fetch

2. Time Out Market
Avenida 24 de Julho 49, Cais do Sodré; www.timeoutmarket.com
///hardens.stumble.copy

3. O Bom O Mau e O Vilão
Rua do Alecrim 21, Cais do Sodré; www.obomomaueovilao.pt
///acute.pebble.tonic

4. B.Leza
Cais do Gás 1, Cais do Sodré; www.bleza.pt
///wiring.erase.styled

5. Titanic Sur Mer
Cais da Ribeira Nova, Cais do Sodré; 938 833 532
///drips.took.declines

📍 **Pink Street**
///remix.tailors.graphic

Watch the sunset from JAVÁ
Enjoy those last rays of sunshine while nursing a cocktail at this rooftop bar.

RUA DOM LUÍS I

PR
D
LU

AVENIDA 24 DE JULHO

Enjoy the beats at B.LEZA
Ready to hit the dancefloor? Move to the rhythms of *kizomba* or *funaná* at this Afrobeats club.

RUA DO ATAÍDE

RUA DO ALECRIM

RUA SÃO PAULO

PRAÇA DE
SÃO PAULO

Raise a glass at
O BOM O MAU E O VILÃO

Join the crowd swaying to the live
music at this cheerful bar named
after the Western *The Good, the
Bad and the Ugly.*

Fuel up at
TIME OUT MARKET

A big night calls for a big meal,
right? Get the gang to order from
different stalls here, so you can
sample a little bit of everything.

2

RUA DA RIBEIRA NOVA

RUA NOVA

DO CARVALHO

RUA DO ALECRIM

3

AVENIDA 24 DE JULHO

*Brothels have been
turned into bars on Rua
Nova do Carvalho,
better known as* **Pink
Street** *due to its 2013
makeover.*

CAIS DO
SODRÉ

CAIS DO
SODRÉ

PRAÇA
EUROPA

5 RUA DA CINTURA DO PORTO DE LISBOA

Party on at
TITANIC SUR MER

Dance until dawn at this
riverside club housed inside
a former fish auction. The
DJs blast out anything from
samba to indie rock.

Rio Tejo

| 0 metres | 100 |
| 0 yards | 100 |

OUTDOORS

Lisboetas spend as much time outside as possible. And who can blame them when they live in one of Europe's sunniest cities and are surrounded by sea and sand?

Green Spaces

When they're not basking in the sun at the nearest beach, locals retreat to the city's parks and gardens. Every Lisboeta has a favourite green space where they go to feel closer to nature.

TAPADA DAS NECESSIDADES

Map 5; Calçada das Necessidades, Alcântara; ///varieties.imparts.pram

Once a private picnic ground for Portuguese royalty (some say Édouard Manet's salacious 1863 painting *Le Déjeuner sur l'herbe* was inspired by one of Tapada das Necessidades' notorious alfresco parties), this green oasis is now open to all. And it's still Lisbon's hottest picnic spot, with its lush lawns, ruined palace and cracking Tejo views inviting groups to settle for an afternoon. Sound romantic? Alcântara couples certainly think so – you'll spy many twosomes on a first date, lolling on the lawn.

JARDIM DA ESTRELA

Map 3; Praça da Estrela, Estrela; ///fade.parties.stewing

The Jardim da Estrela, slap-bang in the middle of Estrela, is always a hub of activity. On any given day you might see mat-clutching yogis gathering by the pond to salute the sun, kids racing onto the

On the first weekend of every month (except January) the garden hosts a lively arts and crafts market. | playground (and parents keeping a watchful eye from the nearby *quiosque*) or an impromptu concert on the bandstand, happily enjoyed by park passersby.

PARQUE FLORESTAL DE MONSANTO

Map 5; Estrada de Monsanto, Benfica; ///mobile.export.icicles

Back in the 1960s, Lisboetas spent their summer holidays camping in Monsanto, where the shady trees and mountain breeze gave some relief from the heat. Today, folks still pitch up (though tents are only allowed in certain areas) to let off steam, cycling up and down the hills, pounding the wooded paths and taking in the glorious views.

PARQUE EDUARDO VII

Map 5; Parque Eduardo VII, Avenida; ///manager.note.nurses

Portugal and Britain have long been allies (the two countries are bonded by the world's oldest military alliance, don't you know), and this park is yet another symbol of their friendship. First known as Parque da Liberdade, it was renamed in honour of English king Edward VII when he visited it in 1903. But this park isn't some stuffy monument to a treaty, it's a much-needed slice of greenery in the city centre. Here, office workers come to stretch their legs, soak up the views from the *miradouro* and check out what's on at Pavilhão Carlos Lopes, the event space on the edge of the park.

» Don't leave without admiring the tropical plants growing in Estufa Fria, the park's stunning greenhouse.

JARDIM DA CERCA DA GRAÇA

Map 1; Calçada do Monte, Graça; ///obeyed.detection.starred

Green spaces are few and far between in the historic centre, so Graça residents rejoiced when this garden opened in 2015, and it soon became a neighbourhood staple. Tumbling down the hill from the Miradouro da Graça, this scrubby patch of green is where friends come to while away those seemingly endless summer days, sprawling across the grass, bottle of beer in hand, and soaking up those enchanting skyline views.

CAMPO DOS MÁRTIRES DA PÁTRIA

Map 4; Campo dos Mártires da Pátria, Arroios; ///modest.digital.sponge

Nestled in the heart of Arroios, this grassy square is a tale of two halves (it's literally split in two by a busy road). The smaller, northern corner is all about helping kids let off steam, with a jungle gym, table tennis tables and a street art-splashed basketball court. Laced with

While shoppers pound Avenida da Liberdade, popping in and out of its pricey boutiques, locals in the know slip past them and climb up to Jardim do Torel. With its shady trees, little plunge pool and pop-up, urban beach, this is one of the best places in Lisbon to escape the summer heat. And as few know of its existence, and even fewer can face the climb in the heat, you should easily nab a good spot on the sand.

paths, and dotted with purple jacaranda trees and duck-filled lakes, the bigger, southern portion of the park, meanwhile, is reserved for the grown-ups, who come seeking a little rest and relaxation.

» Don't leave without grabbing a scoop from nearby Mú. Its vegan piña colada gelato is out of this world.

JARDIM MÁRIO SOARES

Map 6; Campo Grande, Alvalade; ///quality.shorter.gains

Bordering Universidade de Lisboa's main campus, this long and skinny garden is a student fave. But don't go expecting a party vibe. Students grab coffees from the little red *quiosque* (or fast food from the McDonalds in the northern half of the park), before settling on the grass to pour over library books for their next assignments. Join them on the lawn with a good paperback or try your hand at *padel* (a racket game similar to tennis) on the courts.

JARDIM GULBENKIAN

Map 5; Avenida de Berna 45A, Avenidas Novas; ///convert.unique.traps; www.gulbenkian.pt

Jardim Gulbenkian is so much more than a museum garden. It's a hideaway for Avenida Novas' office workers, who flock here to eat their lunch in peace before making a slow lap around the lake. It's an open-air theatre, with its grand amphitheatre hosting concert orchestras, dance troupes and Shakespearean dramas. And come the weekend, it's a quiet reading nook or outdoor yoga studio for locals who like to take their weekends slow.

Scenic City Strolls

Lisbon is a city made for strolling. Head down curious cobbled alleys, pass buildings decorated with azulejos *and street art, and pause at* quiosques *and* miradouros *for as long as you like.*

28 TRAM ROUTE

Map 2; start at Largo Luís de Camões, Chiado; ///replays.marble.wedge

There's a reason why the 28 tram became a hit with tourists – it stops at some of the city's must-see sights and runs along some seriously scenic streets. But why would you want to speed past these views? Follow the tracks on foot instead, taking in *azulejo*-bejewelled and time-faded buildings at your own pace. Every so often, a tinkling bell will signal the approach of the yellow tram and you'll be treated to a kerbside view of this Lisbon icon rolling by.

BAIXA

Map 1; start at Praça do Comércio, Baixa; ///bravest.pens.jeep

When the mercury soars, the whole city seems to hit this downtown neighbourhood for a stroll. Why? Well, for one, it's cooler down here than up in the hills, because of the breeze that builds over the Tejo. And, secondly, there's always something afoot at this time of year in

Getting hungry? Grab a bite to eat at Estação Fluvial Sul e Sueste, a repurposed ferry terminal en route.

Baixa's wide avenues and sun-filled squares, whether it's a fire-breathing street performance or an impromptu music and dance act..

AQUEDUTO DAS ÁGUAS LIVRES

**Map 5; start at Calçada da Quintinha 6, Campolide;
///mailing.bounty.cakes**

When they're out to impress a first date, Lisboetas buy two tickets to walk a 1-km (half-mile) stretch of the Aqueduto das Águas Livres. Standing tall, this 18th-century aqueduct is all about the views: to one side, the quirky area of Amoreiras, with its eye-catching post-modernist buildings; to the other, the lush green hills of Monsanto, with the city's beloved Tejo sparkling beyond.

» Don't leave without extending your date with a walk in Monsanto. The aqueduct ends right on the edge of this wilderness.

AVENIDA DA LIBERDADE

Map 1; start at Praça do Rossio, Avenida; ///recently.native.amused

A hot contender for Lisbon's most scenic boulevard (and, supposedly, the most expensive shopping street in Europe), Avenida da Liberdade stretches between Praça do Rossio and Praça Marquês de Pombal in a wide, straight line. While its boutiques are only for the super-wealthy, all walks of Lisbon life stroll the *avenida's* tree-shaded and intricately patterned *calçadas* (cobblestone pavements), pausing occasionally on a bench to watch the world go by.

GRAÇA

Map 1; start at Miradouro da Graça, Graça; ///renting.pins.rent

Lace up your sturdiest shoes and get ready to work up a sweat, because there's no avoiding Lisbon's famously hilly terrain in the city's highest *bairro*. Graça's killer views are more than worth it, though, and once you've reached the top, you can always hold onto the fact that it's all mercifully downhill from here.

ALFAMA

Map 1; start at Largo da Sé, Alfama; ///brochure.hillside.remit

It's impossible to follow a set route through labyrinthine Alfama. The joy of strolling through this neighbourhood is seeing where your feet will take you. You might end up at the door of a basement fado bar or suddenly come across a *miradouro* that you never knew was there. What's for certain is that you'll fall in love with this neighbourhood, where colourful garlands are strewn above alleys, laundry billows through open windows and no two streets are the same.

» Don't leave without stopping for a shot of *ginjinha*. This is the best place to try the sweet cherry liqueur.

THE TEJO

Map 1; start at Cais das Colunas, Baixa; ///womanly.bind.clings

Lisbon's hills can be a killer on the calves so, when they're after a gentle stroll, locals head to pancake-flat Baixa to walk along the Tejo. With river views all the way, plenty of cute *quiosque* stops and an easy, straight route, it's a no-brainer for a weekend wind-down.

Liked by the locals

"I love walking in Alfama because there are so many narrow, cobbled lanes, steep staircases and secret alleyways just waiting to be discovered. And, of course, you are never far from a nice little café, with alfresco tables, where you can stop and have a coffee."

DIOGO MACEDO, ALFAMA RESIDENT

Dreamy Viewpoints

Okay, it's not true that Lisbon was built on seven hills, but at times it certainly feels like it. The good news? This topography means there are **miradouros** *(viewpoints) all over the city.*

MIRADOURO KEIL DO AMARAL

Map 5; Estrada de Montes Claros, Benfica; ///tabloid.relating.secretly

The trek from the city centre to this *miradouro*, in the corner of the Monsanto hills, is more than worth it. From this hill-meets-amphitheatre, you're afforded great views of Lisbon's two look-alike landmarks: the Ponte 25 de Abril (a dead ringer for San Francisco's Golden Gate Bridge) and the Cristo Rei (inspired by Rio's Christ the Redeemer statue).

» Don't leave without swinging by the *quiosque* to grab a drink and see what's on – it usually hosts live music and DJ sets in the summer.

MIRADOURO DE SANTA LUZIA

Map 1; Largo Santa Luzia, Alfama; ///bats.coasted.guarding

With its vine-draped pergola, blue-and-white *azulejos* and inviting swimming pool, Miradouro de Santa Luzia is picture-perfect. And that's ignoring the stunning views themselves: imagine terracotta

If Santa Luzia is looking pretty crowded, head to nearby Miradouro das Portas do Sol.

roofs, pastel-coloured walls and the sparkling Tejo beyond. If you're after the perfect place to update your social media profiles, this is it.

MIRADOURO DA SENHORA DO MONTE

Map 4; Largo Monte, Graça; ///packages.egging.crib

Legend has it that young lovers used to sneak up to the Miradouro da Senhora do Monte to court without the interference of pesky parents or gossiping neighbours. And maybe it's true – today, this *miradouro* is classic date-spot territory. As the sun turns the sky pink, couples begin the climb up to this, the highest viewpoint in the city. (A tip: take the tram to the nearest stop if you want to avoid huffing and puffing in front of a date.) At the top, they're treated to a sweeping panorama featuring all of the city's major landmarks, from Castelo de São Jorge on its wooded hill in Alfama to Cristo Rei on the other side of the Tejo.

MIRADOURO DO RECOLHIMENTO

Map 1; Rua do Recolhimento, Alfama; ///pinks.tipping.future

While tourists drop some serious cash to see the city from Castelo de São Jorge's battlements, locals ignore the inevitable queue at the ticket booth and head to Miradouro do Recolhimento. On this hidden terrace, a wooden hexagon perfectly frames the view over higgledy-piggledy Alfama to the Mosteiro de São Vicente de Fora and the National Pantheon. *Belíssimo!*

Solo, Pair, Crowd

Whether you're looking for a quiet spot to reflect or a rowdy sunset session, Lisbon has a viewpoint for you.

FLYING SOLO
Take a seat

You could spend hours at Miradouro São Pedro de Alcântara, nursing a *bica* from the *quiosque*, listening to the buskers and reading your book (if you can pull your eyes away from the view, that is).

IN A PAIR
Wine with a view

Ask any Graçaite where to take a date, and they'll direct you to Miradouro da Graça. Nab a seat beside the *quiosque*, order a bottle of wine and get to know each other as you take in the scenes from one of the city's highest hills.

FOR A CROWD
Sunset sounds

Miradouro de Santa Catarina is one of the vibiest places in the city to watch the sun go down. Groups of friends sit on the floor, watching the sky turn from blue to fiery red, while musicians jam in the background.

MIRADOURO DO MONTE AGUDO

Map 4; Rua Heliodoro Salgado, Arroios; ///wing.rummage.films

This tucked-away viewpoint has been a favourite after-work haunt of Arroios residents for years. Grab a beer from the *quiosque*, settle into a beach chair and while away the evening admiring the views stretching across a patchwork of terracotta roofs, all the way to the Tejo.

PANORÂMICO DE MONSANTO

Map 5; Estrada da Bela Vista, Benfica; ///eyelid.rational.pictured

A high-end restaurant, a nightclub, a bingo house: Panorâmico de Monsanto led a series of glamorous lives before it was abandoned in 2001. Street artists soon discovered the pavilion-like building, splashing its interior with graffiti, and tempting intrepid locals to sneak into the site to check out the ever-changing murals and Monsanto views. Today, the Panorâmico is a lot more accessible (it's even got opening hours), but it still flies under the radar.

>> Don't leave without checking out Vhils' mural. Here, he pays tribute to Marielle Franco, a Brazilian politician assassinated in 2018.

PILAR 7

Map 5; Avenida da Índia, Alcântara; ///bond.prongs.deposits; 211 117 880

Riding Lisbon's creeping *elevadores* (funiculars and lifts) will never get old but if you're after a more 21st-century experience, head to Pilar 7. Here, a glass-bottomed lift glides you up the side of Ponte 25 de Abril for jaw-to-floor views over the glittering Tejo.

By the Water

Lisbon's history is intertwined with the Atlantic, and it continues to play a big part in Lisboetan life today. In their downtime, locals head straight to their favourite beach to surf, swim and sunbathe.

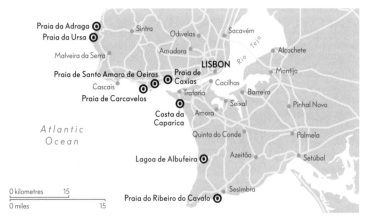

PRAIA DE CARCAVELOS

40-minute train ride from Cais do Sodré; ///speaker.climbing.views

Buffeted by wild, Atlantic waves and blessed with seemingly endless sunshine, Portugal is a surfer's paradise, and the sport has become a national obsession. Even on one of Lisbon's few cloudy days, *surfistas* grab their boards and head out to Praia de Carcavelos.

Here, they catch some waves before warming up in one of the beachfront cafés or restaurants. Beginners will find several surf schools here, guaranteed (well, fingers crossed) to have you standing up by the end of the class.

» Don't leave without making the 20-minute walk to Piscina Oceânica de Oeiras, a large salt-water pool with diving boards.

COSTA DA CAPARICA

40-minute bus ride from Sete Rios or Alcântara;
///weekends.channel.probe

Lisboetas' summertime exodus to the Costa da Caparica inspired 1980s punk rockers Peste & Sida's hit "Sol da Caparica". And on scorching days, it seems like the whole city has crossed the Ponte 25 de Abril and set up camp on this coast's 30 km (19 miles) of sand. Excited kids splash about in the shallows, friends hit the waves on surfboards and parents sunbathe on beach towels.

PRAIA DA URSA

1-hour bus ride from Sintra or Cascais; ///openly.seriousness.liberally

Only the most serious of sunseekers are willing to make the steep schlep to this secluded cove. Their reward is only a slither of sand, encircled by craggy cliffs, but they're almost guaranteed to have it to themselves. This privacy makes it unsurprisingly popular with local skinny dippers and nude sunbathers, who spend the day paddling in the shallow water and relaxing on the sand, before braving the hike back to the real world.

PRAIA DA ADRAGA

1-hour bus ride from Sintra, plus 30-minute walk;
///horn.unexplained.accumulates

As wonderful as Lisbon's *miradouros* are, you can't beat the beach when it comes to sunset scenes. And Praia da Adraga provides some of the best: here, groups linger to watch the sinking sun turn the beach a pinky mauve, then copper red, while the rocks out to sea become pitch black against the sky. Once the show's over, it's off to Restaurante da Adraga for fresh clams poached in white wine.

LAGOA DE ALBUFEIRA

40-minute drive from Lisbon; ///internship.compendium.pillowcases

You know you've arrived at Lagoa de Albufeira when you spot the colourful kites dancing in the sky. Blessed with a blustery breeze, but sheltered from the Atlantic swell, this lagoon is plied by kitesurfers and paddleboarders. Prefer dry land? All this activity creates a fine backdrop for catch-up strolls along the banks to Praia da Lagoa de Albufeira-Mar, where the lagoon meets the sea.

Try it!
LEARN TO SURF

Impressed by the high-flying moves of Lagoa de Albufeira's kitesurfers? Book onto a beginners class with Meira Procenter *(en. meiraprocenter.com)*. You might not master a flip, but you'll get into the air.

PRAIA DO RIBEIRO DO CAVALO

45-minute bus ride from Lisbon; ///hurdled.cheaper.incomplete

With its crystal-clear waters, lush green hills and golden sweep of sand, Praia do Ribeiro do Cavalo exudes serious postcard vibes. Keeping things real, there are no amenities whatsoever at this paradisal spot, accessed via a steep track, so come prepared with drinks and snacks.

PRAIA DE CAXIAS

15-minute train ride from Cais do Sodré; ///market.blanks.going

On days when they just can't face getting out of bed early and trekking out to a far-away beach, Lisboetas snooze their alarms and decide to go to Caxias instead. Set where the Tejo opens up into the Atlantic, this golden sweep of sand is so close to the city that you can spy Ponte 25 de Abril and Cristo Rei. Sun, sand and city views? It's a no-brainer.

» Don't leave without swinging by Bahia Beach Club for some Brazilian tunes and a refreshing bowl of açai.

PRAIA DE SANTO AMARO DE OEIRAS

25-minute train ride from Cais do Sodré; ///unwanted.rift.brighter

Every Lisboeta has a favourite beach, and for students at the Universidade de Lisboa, it's got to be Santo Amaro. It's just a short walk from the train station (welcome news when you're laden down with a cooler full of beer) and it's wide enough for the whole gang to play beach games. Time seems to stretch here, a bit like those long teenage summers you can just about remember.

Nearby Getaways

Lisboetas wouldn't choose to live anywhere else, but that doesn't mean that they never leave their beloved city. Every once in a while, they strike out to explore a nearby beach or chocolate-box town for the day.

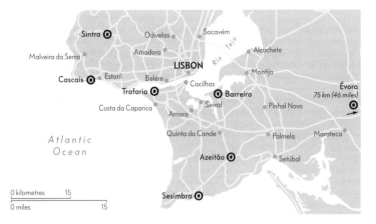

AZEITÃO

1 hour bus ride from Alcântara; www.visitsetubal.com

It's no secret: Lisboetas love their food and drink, which is exactly why they make the trip to Azeitão on the regular. This teeny town is known for three things – its eponymous cheese (a deliciously smelly and creamy variety), Moscatel (a sweet fortified wine) and *torta de*

Take the five-minute drive to Quinta de Alcube, on the edge of town, for a cheese-paired wine tasting.

azeitão (a sweet sponge-cake-like roll, filled with custard). Get your fill at Pastelaria Cego, which bakes the best in town.

ÉVORA

90-minute train ride from Sete Rios; www.visitalentejo.pt

The perfect weekend destination? It's got to be Évora. This UNESCO-listed city's historic sights undoubtedly hog the headlines. First off, there's the Roman temple, dating from the 1st century AD. Then, there's Igreja de São Francisco and its Capela dos Ossos, an eerie chapel covered with thousands of bones (yes, really). But that's not all that this Alentejan city has to offer – it's surrounded by tumbling vineyards and wild beaches that are made for Sunday strolling.

SESIMBRA

45-minute bus ride from Sete Rios; www.visitsesimbra.pt

There's one big reason to head to Sesimbra: the seafood. Set in a sheltered bay at the foot of the Arrábida hills, this seaside town revolves around its fishing industry. There's a fortress-turned-museum dedicated to Sesimbra's fisherfolk, and locals even call themselves *"pexitos"* (little fish). Unsurprisingly, the area is awash with restaurants serving up just-caught seafood.

≫ Don't leave without walking the steep, winding trail to Ribeiro do Cavalo *(p179)*. With its white sands, jutting rock formations and turquoise waters, this beach is as close to paradise as it gets.

CASCAIS

45-minute train ride from Cais do Sodré; www.visitcascais.com

Back in the 19th century, Cascais was the most fashionable place in the country to try sea bathing. Portuguese royalty and nobility flocked to this small seaside town to roll into the water in their bathing machines, and the Duke and Duchess of Palmela even built a grand palace right on the bay. These days, all walks of life take to the waters — and make the most of the town's excellent exhibitions, boutiques and bars, too.

TRAFARIA

20-minute ferry ride from Belém; www.visitportugal.com

Although it's only a hop, skip and a ferry ride from the city, Trafaria seems a world away from Lisbon's hustle and bustle. And it's exactly where weary office workers go for a bit of R&R come the weekend. Nothing blows the cobwebs away like a windswept walk along the

Few people bother to make the 30-minute walk from Trafaria to Cova do Vapor, and this tiny fishing village is all the better for it. The beach is practically deserted, the waterfront bars always have spare seats and prices are wonderfully wallet-friendly, which isn't always true of its more popular neighbour. While you're sitting in that bar, order a Cai Bem, the village's signature drink (*ginjinha*, soda and lemon juice).

beach, past cute-as-a-button whitewashed cottages on one side and bobbing fishing boats on the other. Watching the sun set over Belém from a waterside bar doesn't hurt either.

SINTRA

1-hour train ride from Rossio; www.visitsintra.travel

Most people picture the Palácio Nacional da Pena when they hear Sintra. Like something straight out of a twisted fairytale, this mishmash of colourful towers and domes has captured the world's imagination. But most locals give it, and Sintra's many other palaces, a wide berth, rather donning their walking boots and heading out into Serra de Sintra, a vast, untamed mountain range. Join them on the trails and you'll soon discover why English poet Lord Byron likened this landscape to the garden of Eden.

>> Don't leave without trying a *travesseiro*, a delicious puff pastry with a sweet almond and egg yolk filling. Casa Piriquita, slap-bang in the centre of town, makes some of the best.

BARREIRO

25-minute ferry ride from Terreiro do Paço; www.cm-barreiro.pt

If Lisbon's coolest had to live anywhere else, they'd choose Barreiro, "the Brooklyn of Lisbon". And it certainly lives up to its nickname. Just like its American cousin, this once run-down industrial town is now a hipster hub, buzzing with craft breweries, vegan cafés and an enviable street art scene (superstar street artist Vhils has already made the move here).

An afternoon exploring
Alfama's viewpoints

Ah, Alfama! There's something magical about the city's oldest neighbourhood. In this maze of Moorish streets, you'll stumble upon little *tabernas*, where fado was first sung centuries ago, and *miradouros*, from which the city unfurls in a patchwork of terracotta roofs, pastel façades and church spires. The only downside to those views? The hills. Luckily, there are plenty of places to pause, often with a drink in hand, along the way. (Or, you could always ride the tram.)

1. Miradouro da Graça
Calçada da Graça, Graça
///renting.pins.rent

2. Miradouro das Portas do Sol
Largo Portas do Sol, Alfama
///puppy.frocks.rarely

3. Miradouro de Santa Luzia
Largo Santa Luzia, Alfama
///bats.coasted.guarding

4. Miradouro do Recolhimento
Rua do Recolhimento, Alfama
///pinks.tipping.future

5. Castelo de São Jorge
Rua de Santa Cruz do Castelo, Mouraria; www.castelodesaojorge.pt
///exhaled.expand.ants

 Calçada ///critic.embedded.restless

 28 tram ///tiny.bolts.airports

RUA DOS CAVALEIRO

PRAÇA MARTIM MONIZ

MOURARIA

Catch the sunset at CASTELO DE SÃO JORGE
After meandering around its perimeter, head into the castle grounds in time to watch the sun slip beneath the battlements.

RUA DA MADALENA

BAIXA

RUA DA CONCEIÇÃO

GRAÇA

Jardim da Cerca da Graça

Ride up to
MIRADOURO DA GRAÇA
Take the 28 tram to Miradouro da Graça for breathtaking views of the castle and the Tejo river.

1

LARGO DA GRAÇA

CALÇADA DE SANTO ANDRÉ

CALÇADA DA GRAÇA

COSTA DO CASTELO

LARGO RODRIGUES DE FREITAS

*Designed by street artist Vhils, **Calçada** is a portrait of local fado singer Amália Rodrigues, made up of mosaicked cobblestones.*

Rest up at
MIRADOURO DO RECOLHIMENTO
It's quite a steep climb up to this viewpoint, but we promise it's worth it. Stay a while to drink in the incredible views – and catch your breath.

RUA DE SÃO TOMÉ

Stroll down to
MIRADOURO DAS PORTAS DO SOL
Order a refreshing glass of *vinho verde* from the *quiosque* and soak up the Alfama scenes.

SANTO ESTÊVÃO

4

RUA DO CHÃO DA FEIRA

TRAVESSA DO FUNIL

2

LARGO DAS PORTAS DO SOL

ALFAMA

RUA DOS REMÉDIOS

LARGO DOS LÓIOS

*The **28 tram** ferries people up and down Alfama's hills, taking in some of the city's most scenic streets along the way.*

3

Get under cover at
MIRADOURO DE SANTA LUZIA
Escape the sun under the shady pergola, which is draped in romantic bougainvillea between spring and autumn, and admire the *azulejos* that decorate the walls.

AVENIDA INFANTE DOM HENRIQUE

LARGO DA SÉ

| 0 metres | 200 |
| 0 yards | 200 |

With a little research and preparation, this city will feel like a home away from home. Check out these websites to ensure a healthy, safe stay in Lisbon.

Lisbon

DIRECTORY

SAFE SPACES

Lisbon is a welcoming city, but if you feel uneasy at any point or want to find your community, there are plenty of supportive spaces. Here are just a handful.

www.amcv.org.pt
Nonprofit resource offering support, advice and shelter for women and young people affected by any form of violence.

www.comunidadeislamica.pt
The CIL (Comunidade Islâmica de Lisboa), headquartered at Lisbon Central Mosque, is the focal point of Portugal's Islamic community.

www.lgbt.pt
Nonprofit organization running events and offering support for Lisbon's LGBTQ+ community.

www.proudlyportugal.pt
A curated online guide to Lisbon's LGBTQ+-friendly sights and experiences.

HEALTH

Healthcare in Portugal isn't free to all so make sure you have comprehensive insurance; emergency healthcare is covered by the European Health Insurance Card (EHIC) for EU residents and the UK Global Health Insurance Card (GHIC) for those from the UK. If you do need medical assistance, there are many pharmacies and hospitals.

www.checkpointlx.com
Nonprofit organization providing free sexual health care for all.

www.farmaciasdeservico.net
A comprehensive list of pharmacies, searchable by neighbourhood.

www.sns24.gov.pt

Portugal's national health service website provides around-the-clock advice and referrals, and a comprehensive list of hospitals and health centres in Lisbon and the surrounding area.

TRAVEL SAFETY ADVICE

Lisbon is by and large a safe city. Before you travel – and while you're here – it's worth brushing up on the latest regulations and security measures.

www.apav.pt

Charity offering help and advice for victims of any type of crime in Portugal, including how to report an incident and access health care.

www.portugalcleanandsafe.com

Up-to-date information on COVID-19 regulations and pandemic-safe travel.

www.safecommunitiesportugal.com

English-language resource offering extensive information on keeping safe and reporting crimes in Lisbon and further afield.

www.visitlisboa.com

Inspirational and practical information, and advice on all things Lisbon from the city's official tourism board.

ACCESSIBILITY

Lisbon has come a long way when it comes to accessibility, but all those hills and medieval streets can prove tricky for wheelchair users, and some places may be lacking in facilities. It's always best to check ahead.

www.aeroportolisboa.pt

Passengers with reduced mobility can use Lisbon international airport's free MyWay assistance service to get around the airport (book in advance).

www.metrolisboa.pt/en/travel/ diagrams-and-maps/

A downloadable map of accessible metro stations in Lisbon.

www.tourism-for-all.com

Travel agency and tour operator specializing in accessible travel in Portugal.

www.tur4all.com/pt/home

A comprehensive list of venues, restaurants, attractions and travel bodies that are accessible to all.

www.visitportugal.com/en/content/ accessible-beach

A list of accessible beaches located all around Portugal.

INDEX

ABOUT THE ILLUSTRATOR

Mantas Tumosa

*Creative designer and illustrator Mantas
moved from his home country of Lithuania
to London back in 2011. By day, he's busy
creating bold, minimalistic illustrations that
tell a story – such as the gorgeous cover of
this book. By night, he's dreaming of
adventures away, catching up on the
basketball and cooking Italian food (which
he can't get enough of).*

Main Contributors Joana Taborda,
Lucy Bryson, Reuben Ross
Senior Editor Lucy Richards
Senior Designers Tania Gomes, Ben Hinks
Project Editor Rebecca Flynn
Project Art Editor Bharti Karakoti
Designer Jordan Lambley
Proofreader Stephanie Smith
Senior Cartographic Editor Casper Morris
Cartography Manager Suresh Kumar
Cartographer Ashif
Jacket Designer Tania Gomes, Jordan Lambley
Jacket Illustrator Mantas Tumosa
Senior Production Editor Jason Little
Production Controller Samantha Cross
Managing Editor Hollie Teague
Managing Art Editor Sarah Snelling
Art Director Maxine Pedliham
Publishing Director Georgina Dee

First edition 2022
Published in Great Britain by Dorling Kindersley Limited,
DK, One Embassy Gardens, 8 Viaduct Gardens,
London SW11 7BW, UK
The authorised representative in the EEA is
Dorling Kindersley Verlag GmbH. Arnulfstr.
124, 80636 Munich, Germany
Published in the United States by DK Publishing,
1745 Broadway, 20th Floor, New York, NY 10019, USA

Copyright © 2022 Dorling Kindersley Limited
A Penguin Random House Company
22 23 24 25 10 9 8 7 6 5 4 3 2 1

The publishers cannot accept responsibility for any consequences arising from
the use of this book, nor for any material on third party websites, and cannot
guarantee that any website address in this book will be a suitable source of
travel information.
A CIP catalog record for this book is available from the British Library.
A catalog record for this book is available from the Library of Congress.
ISSN: 1542 1554
ISBN: 9780 2415 6827 9
Printed and bound in China.
www.dk.com

A NOTE FROM DK EYEWITNESS

The world is fast-changing and it's keeping us folk at
DK Eyewitness on our toes. We've worked hard to ensure
that this edition of Lisbon Like a Local is up-to-date and
reflects today's favourite places but we know that standards
shift, venues close and new ones pop up in their place. So, if
you notice something has closed, we've got something
wrong or left something out, we want to hear about it.
Drop us a line at travelguides@dk.com